The Sausage Book

BY RICHARD GEHMAN

Novels
A Party at the Buchanan Club
Driven
The Slander of Witches
The Had

Non-Fiction
A Murder in Paradise
How To Write and Sell Magazine Articles
Let My Heart Be Broken
The Barking Rabbit

Collaborations
Sardi's (with Vincent Sardi, Sr.)
The Jury Is Still Out (with Judge Irwin D. Davidson)
Eddie Condon's Treasury of Jazz (with Eddie Condon)
A Hell of a Life (with Harry Richman)

Juvenile
The Tall American

Biographies
Sinatra and His Rat Pack
That Kid: The Story of Jerry Lewis
Bogart

Cookbooks
The Haphazard Gourmet
In the Soup, in a Stew
The Sausage Book

The Sausage Book

Being a compendium

of

SAUSAGE RECIPES,

Ways of
making and eating sausage,
accompanying dishes,
and strong waters to be served.
Including many recipes from
Germany, France, and Lancaster County,
Pennsylvania,
and committed to paper
by

RICHARD GEHMAN

Weathervane Books • New York

For Gerald, Margaret,
Sally Dana, Michael E., Robert Dana
and Linda Lestz;
and in the memory of Edith Lestz,
who, before her death put much cheer into the lives
of those of us who knew and treasured her.
For all these dear people, I dedicate this book,
which in places may not be suitable for the perusal
of the younger ones.

CONTENTS

The Sausage Book

A Sausage by Any Name

In Greenwich Village, many years ago, I used to know a man named Charles Caruso, a hard-working Italian with a bearish, brusque voice that in no way resembled that of the great Italian tenor of the same last name. Nevertheless, Charles was every inch the artist that Enrico Caruso was. Nearly every day around noon, Charles would go into his studio on Carmine Street and grind up pork butts and scraps, season the grindings with salt and strong black pepper and a couple of herbs—the names of which he never would divulge—and stuff the resulting redolent mixture into an animal casing to make *salsiccia dolce*, or sweet sausage.

By the time he made about 50 pounds of short, fat sausages, it would be nearly dusk. Charles carried his sausages, plus several gallons of stewed peppers, previously prepared by his wife, out to a large iron-roofed pushcart parked near the curb. This cart, constructed of sheet metal to his own specifications, was Charles' pride and joy. It was equipped with a grill, compartments to keep the peppers warm, and a small stove to relieve Charles' accursed arthritis in winter. He trundled the cart a couple of blocks north to the busy subway-stop corner of West Third Street and Sixth Avenue. There he climbed into the cart, lighted a fire under his grill, and placed on it a succulent coil of *salsiccia dolce*.

Within a few seconds, the sausages began to snarl, spit and buzz, sending out a wonderfully magnetic odor. A customer would step up and demand one. Charles would cut a single sausage from the coil, split it neatly in half and press it down on the grill, browning its insides before placing it on a soft

1

fresh roll. He added a large spoonful of the simmering peppers, sprinkled the sausage with dried red pepper seeds, wrapped it neatly in a paper napkin, handed it to the customer and collected 35 cents. Meanwhile, the mingled smell of sausages and peppers attracted more people. It even drew some of Charles' neighbors up from Carmine Street. It drew me, too.

I am a sausage fool. A long time ago, I fell shamelessly in love with this ancient, delicious example of man's imaginative mastery of foodstuffs.

Sausage is man's meat—strong-flavored, full of character, honestly designed for hearty eaters. It is woman's meat, too. The beauty of sausage is that in various forms it can be eaten almost any time—for breakfast, with eggs; for lunch, with sauerkraut and mashed or boiled potatoes; for dinner, in a number of excellent casseroles; and for late night poker games or pre-bed sandwiches. And, of course, it can be eaten between meals in the form of the frankfurter. Babe Ruth, according to legend, frequently knocked off 10 or 12 hot dogs during the seventh-inning stretch.

During the past years I have been having the time of my life, eating sausage while researching this book, watching it being made, and talking to the men who make it. I have watched these sausage-mixers go furtively into their storerooms with a small scoop to blend the herbs and spices in utmost secret, and I have begged sausage recipes from the masters, who are the Germans. They are considered to be the greatest artists in this fascinating business.

The Germans do not have a corner on the sausage market. I have eaten not only German sausage, but also Italian, Ukrainian, Greek, Spanish, Chinese, Dutch and French sausage. I have eaten sausage dry, cooked and smoked. I have eaten sausages so moist they could be spread with a pliable knife, and sausages hard as marbles. I have eaten sausages made of beef, pork, veal, tongue, liver and other innards, and flavored with pepper, cumin, dill, fennel, mace, parsley and many other herbs and spices as well as sausages tinged with orange peel and steeped in wine.

2

There are more than 100 varieties of sausage made and eaten in the United States. Even the big meat manufacturers hesitate to say exactly how many. E. L. Hecker of Armour Company told me, "We make over 100 different ones ourselves. Most of our sausage is made in local sausage kitchens, and their products vary to meet local preferences as to style, casing, spicing, coloring and packaging." A master sausage maker, Ferdinand Schaller of New York, estimated that there are more than 500 different kinds of sausage being made and eaten the world around, and, in the same breath, he admitted that his figure is probably low.

The reason there are so many kinds lies in the definition of sausage, which is a loose term. The American Meat Institute defines it as "A mixture of meat, usually ground, and other foodstuffs, in a natural or artificial casing or tube." There are six major categories of sausage:

FRESH: Made from meats that have not been cooked or cured—fresh pork sausage, for example; *weisswurst, bratwurst* or *bockwurst.*

SMOKED: Made from cured meats and other ingredients and smoked over wood fires. There are two kinds of smoked sausage, cooked smoked, which includes frankfurters, bologna and *mortadella;* and uncooked smoked, which includes smoked pork sausage and *mettwurst.*

COOKED: Made from fresh or cured meat and cooked in the casings—liverwurst, blood sausage, etc.

NEW CONDITIONED: Made of ground meats to which spices and curing agents are added, after which the sausage is cured for several days before being smoked. This category includes cooked salamis, cervelats, and Kosher salamis.

DRY: Made from fresh meats to which spices are added, after which the sausage is cured for days and then dried in the air under special conditions for long periods of time. Italian dry salamis are in this class, plus such German products as *holsteiner, landjaeger* and *gothaer;* also Spanish sausages, called *chorizos.*

COOKED SPECIALTIES: This is the catch-all category, and includes almost anything that is put in a casing.

Technically speaking, head cheese, which is made of bits of pig's head meat cooked and allowed to cool and jell, is sausage because it is stuffed into a casing or tube. So are blood puddings, popular in many countries, especially in Britain. In Scotland, blood pudding is made of blood, oatmeal, onions and other spices, encased in a sheep's stomach, and called *haggis*. So, too, is *metzelsuppe* (scrap soup), a Pennsylvania Dutch dish consisting of ground pork scraps, potatoes, cabbage, onions and bread all crammed into a pig's stomach, which is baked or boiled and sliced down for serving. As far as that goes, even *gänsebrust* could be considered a sausage-family member. *Gänsebrust* is smoked goose breast wrapped with a casing of goose skin.

The casings, or tubes, into which sausage meat is stuffed are usually the intestines, or bowels, of sheep, hogs or cattle. Sausage-makers are remarkably frank in speaking of the casings. "From one steer, I get 30 yards of beef rounds, or intestines, 10 yards of the middle intestines, and one yard of beef bung," says Ferdinand Schaller.

Beef intestines are used for sausages that require thicker casings, such as liverwursts and bolognas. Sheep intestines are used for frankfurters, principally, but, beginning about 30 years ago, the nation's sheep kill was not equal to the demand for hot dog casings. Therefore, artificial casings made from cellulose were introduced. The casings were stripped off after the frankfurters were precooked by the manufacturers, resulting in the "skinless" frankfurter. The practice grieved the old-line sausage manufacturers. They state candidly that the skinless kind are not as good as the "bunged" ones. A sausage, these craftsmen say, ought to have a natural casing because a casing keeps in the juices while the meat is being cooked. Also, intestines add immensely to the flavor of the sausage.

Innards are not the only casings that sausage makers use. Some bolognas are wrapped in strong cloth bags which seal in

4

the rich flavor; some are put in skin from which the bristles or hair has been scraped; and some Italian salamis come to this country coated by paraffin. Casing is a big business. New York is not noted for its meat-packing industry, but there are over 40 sausage-casing firms in its classified directory.

Sausage itself is even bigger business. Last year, according to a spokesman for Swift and Company, Americans wolfed down over 3,500,000,000 pounds of federally-inspected sausage. We imported more than 1,500,000 pounds. God alone knows how many millions of pounds were produced in uninspected plants. The fact that some plants were not federally inspected does not mean that their sausage was necessarily impure or imperfect; it simply means that the law says that uninspected sausage cannot be transported across state lines. Some of the best and purest pork sausage made comes from small country butcher shops that turn out only a couple of hundred pounds per week. While not federally inspected, they are supervised closely by state or municipal authorities.

Right here, let us get rid of the old, mistaken notion that sausage is made from undesirable parts of meat, cast-off scraps, sweepings or leavings.

This nonsense amuses or enrages the average sausage-maker, depending upon his temperament. It is true that meat cutters have a hell of a time properly cutting out meat from shoulders, rumps, etc., used in sausage. But most of the time, they cut those small pieces from extra-high-quality parts. Sausage-makers select their meat with the same loving care that the proprietor of a first-class steak house uses to get sirloins that can be cut with a butter knife. But what is high-quality for ordinary consumption is not necessarily high-quality for sausage. When you eat a steak, you try to get one that comes from a steer. When you eat beef sausage, you are eating meat from a tough, ornery bull. Steer meat—grassfed—is too soft for sausage. Bull meat is more fibrous. The two are indistinguishable as to flavor but you can chew steer meat more easily. You can chew bull meat easily, too, once it's been ground up and made into sausage.

5

Sensitive people sometimes object to sausage because they feel that it's made from "castoff" parts of an animal. Blood, intestines, liver, various other innards, plus tongue and foot and cheek meat are used commonly in many varieties of sausage. But all sausage shops, as noted above, are regulated by rigid sanitary codes, and every sausage-maker I've ever met— and I've met scores—takes pride in the excellence of his work and the quality of his product. Actually, sausage is one of the few food products that is almost totally edible, with no waste. It is not expensive, but, because it is *all* edible, it is one of the most economical of all foods as well as one of the tastiest.

We like frankfurters best in America. After them, we like bologna best. Then, fresh pork sausage, meat loaves of various kinds, liverwurst, salami and other dry sausages, in that order.

Sausage is one of the oldest foods known to man. Nobody knows who first thought of stuffing ground-up meat into a sheath, but Homer sang of sausage in the Odyssey, which was written (they say) about 850 B.C. The Babylonians made and ate it, too. The word "salami' supposedly comes from the Greek island of Salamis, where that variety is said to have originated. Our word sausage stems from the Latin *salsus*, the word for salted or preserved meat. The Romans had a sausage made of ground pork and pine nuts, which they especially enjoyed during the *Lupercalia* and the *Floralia*, two pagan orgies of feasting, boozing and wenching which so shocked the pious Constantine, the first Christian emperor, that he banned both holidays and the sausage as well. Even in those days, no emperor's edict could stop a sausage lover and Roman sausage bootleggers sold their wares despite the ban.

Historians state that sausage-making really came into flower along with knighthood, in the Middle Ages. Sausages peculiar to certain cities were named after them: Bologna, from Bologna, Italy; Gothaer, from Gotha, Germany; Romano, from Rome, and so on. When the first colonists got to America, they discovered that the Indians had discovered sausage all by themselves. They had mixed chopped and dried meat with dried berries and pressed the mixture into a cake, which they then

6

smoked and dried further and stacked away against days of hunger.

To the serious sausage student, the makers' silence may be both unscientific and reprehensible, but it is understandable. Sausage-makers are constantly trying to copy their rivals' products—as witness the war between Christ Kunzler, a Lancaster, Pennsylvania, manufacturer, and Eugene Strabley, a Dallastown, Pennsylvania, butcher. The latter had devised an all-beef bologna, long-cured and smoked and spiced with pepper and other condiments, which he called York County Butcher Bologna. Kunzler and his employees spent 25 years trying to duplicate the recipe. They even bought cows from Strabley's neighborhood. Old Strabley sat over there in York cocking a snook. Eventually his health forced him to retire. Hats in hands, the Kunzler people asked him to sell his secret, which he was glad to do for something like $25,000.

The Kunzler firm has a recipe of its own that none of its Lancaster County rivals has ever been able to reproduce satisfactorily—the formula for bockwurst, a white German sausage made from fine-ground beef, pork and veal, blended with eggs and milk and flavored heavily with chives.

Christ Kunzler brought the recipe with him from Baden-Baden, Germany, over 60 years ago. The secret, Christ Jr., hinted to me, is in knowing how to put in the chives, and he implied that there was something special about the chives themselves, which he grows in his own hothouse.

Most sausage-makers take great pride in their work. "I am *artiste*," said Platon Stasiuk, who ran a pork store at 124 First Avenue in New York. Stasiuk, a small man with bristling, close-cut gray hair, came from Eastern Galicia in 1912. He made Ukrainian, Polish and Russian sausages. He also made elaborate window displays. His American flag was magnificent. "From meat! Round steak for red stripes, suet for white stripes and stars, and blue-dyed pork jelly for field. Is artistic?"

Was artistic, I agreed. Later, when Stasiuk gave me some of his *krakowska* to taste, I agreed even more heartily. *Krakowska* is one of the best cold sausages I ever have tasted. Ukrainian in origin, it is made from the tenderest meat on a pork shoulder; even the most monstrous pig does not have more than five or six pounds of this tender meat on him. Stasiuk flavored the meat with pepper, salt, mace, caraway seeds and garlic powder. Then he smoked it in his huge ovens for several days. What came out was unbelievable. With thin-sliced salted rye bread, *krakowska* can be one of the great hors d'oeuvres of all time.

After I communicated my feverish respect for the *krakowska*, Stasiuk put on a furry gray felt hat and, with pride increasing with his every deliberate step, he led me downstairs to his cold-storage room. Here, pork shoulders and sides of bacon lay in a curing brine in huge barrels, awaiting their turns in the smoking ovens. On racks before me were hundreds of orange-red sausages that looked like two-foot hot dogs.

"This is *good*," said Stasiuk positively, pulling down one of the long sausages. "Is called *kabanos*. Is Polish and Ukrainian. Mainly smoked pork, a little beef mixed in. Also wery good with cocktails." He broke off a piece and handed it to me, and I savored the mace and garlic. "And this," he said, taking down a wrist-thick, horseshoe-shaped sausage, "is *sardelowa*. Is also Polish. Seventy-five percent pork, rest beef and veal. You eat it hot. Steam it in a pot, with a little water, not too much or she absorbs the taste. A half-inch of water only. Good with sauerkraut or potatoes."

I asked Stasiuk why some sausages are slightly curved, some curved like horseshoes, and some almost straight.

"Depends on casing," he said. "Casing from beef rounds, pork rounds, upper part of intestines—it curves naturally. Lower intestines are straighter for some reason. Also, tying at the ends has something to do with it. Tighter they tied, more they curve. Smoked sausages are tied tighter than fresh to keep juices in during smoking."

"Who determines the shapes?" I asked.

He shrugged. "Were determined by sausage-makers hundreds of years ago. Is general rule, better a sausage keeps, bigger its shape. You can keep big bologna or big salami long time, so is made big. Small fresh sausage, wery perishable, is made small. Same way with frankfurters."

We started upstairs and passed a room where thick, shiny black sausages were hanging. "Is *kishka*," Stasiuk said. "Russian. Made of fat trimmings, groats, salt and pepper, chopped onions and, mainly, blood. You need strong stomach for that. Myself, I prefer honest piece of meat. But *kishka* is cheap, and lots of people like." We had some. It is a strong-tasting sausage, salty with blood, the kind of meat that sticks to the teeth and makes the eater believe he is getting stronger as it goes down his throat.

"Now, let me tell you something," Stasiuk continued. "Myself, I am good sausage-maker. I learn from my father. He from his. I know how to butcher, to cut up meat, to build fires in smokehouse, and how to eat. Making sausage is art. But if you want to talk to real sausage-makers, go up to Yorkville and see the Germans."

After eating his *krakowska*, I would have gone to Malaya if he had asked me. But before going to Yorkville, I stopped by to see some friends, the Manganaro brothers, who run the oldest Italian delicatessen in New York City, at 488 Ninth Avenue. They handle 25 or 30 varieties of Italian sausages and salamis, some imported and some domestic.

Vince Manganaro spouted information rapidly. "Most fresh Italian sausage is made in three-inch lengths—sweet and hot," he said. "Very perishable. Most Italian delicatessens or pork stores or groceries make their own, a little at a time. That's the kind your pal in the Village, Caruso, makes. Italian salami is mostly lean pork, chopped coarsely, with some lean beef, chopped finely, and whole grains of pepper added, then dried for many weeks. That, too, is often made at home, but the big companies like Hormel can make it so you can't tell the difference.

"Then, there's *capicolla*, sometimes spelled *cappo collo*, which is boneless pork shoulder, spiced with red pepper and put in a casing—not chopped, but pressed. Very popular, very tasty. The third major type is *mortadella*—well-chopped cubes of beef and pork with fat added. Oh, I forgot *pepperoni*—like salami, but with more pork, dried a very long time, in small thin strips. And with more spices."

Vince paused. "I tell you what," he said, echoing Platon Stasiuk, "If you want to talk to somebody who *knows* sausage, go talk to the Germans. The French are supposed to be the best cooks in the world, and they have a pretty good sausage made out of white meat of chicken, yolk of eggs, crumbs, salt and pepper and parsley and chives. They boil that in the casing, then grill or broil it. They call it *boudin blanc*. But for the best sausage, you *got* to go to the Germans."

That was what I did.

I went to the corner of 86th Street and Second Avenue, to the magnificent shop called Schaller and Weber. It is a small room, measuring only about 12 by 18 feet. The visitor, entering, is first assailed by a delicious smoky haze so strong it will be clinging to his clothes when he leaves. Then he sees the sausages themselves, row upon tantalizing row of them, hanging from the ceiling, from iron crossbars, from the walls. Fat little russet *bauernwurst* and *knockwurst* hanging in strings, great long *braunschweiger leberwurst,* hard thin ropes of red-brown *landjaeger*. And, in the two glass cases, are piles upon piles of fresh pink pork sausages, white veal sausages, three varieties of frankfurters, head cheeses, liverwursts, *blutwursts, bockwursts,* wursts of every size and description. The shop offers 52 varieties, all made in the kitchen in the rear.

Between 15 and 20 men work in the kitchen, depending upon the season. Christmas is Schaller and Weber's big rush period, and then there may be as many as 30 men in the large, tile-floored room. These men, expert as surgeons, can bone a ham in less than one minute and cut up a shoulder into sausage-meat parts in less than two. They are huge, cheerful men with knotty muscles in their arms and flecks of fresh animal blood on their faces and white aprons. Most of them learned their trade from their fathers and are contemptuous of butcher-schools.

Ferdinand Schaller, born in Stuttgart, Germany, about sixty years ago, began making sausages when he was fourteen. "I first worked as an apprentice," he said, "and got paid one mark for the first year, two for the second, three for the third." Schaller was a husky man with a mane of gray hair and clear

10

blue eyes—the picture of the jolly, affable butcher. He opened the store 20 years ago in partnership with Anton Weber, whom he met when they were both working for the large sausage products concern, Stahl-Meyer. They started modestly, but in no time at all they were making more than 25 varieties, all from recipes they had brought from Germany. A few years ago, Weber sold out to Schaller, but the latter continued to expand and now owns five branch stores and a plant on Long Island.

Schaller personally selects all his own meat for the 20,000 pounds of sausage he makes each week. He rises at 4 A.M. two days each week and goes to market. When he returns he takes a hand in all preparations—grinding, chopping, mixing, flavoring with herbs and spices, and cooking the sausages that must be cooked. He also personally eats a good deal of his own products. Each day around noon, he and his meat cutters and clerks sit down to a huge round platter of sausage, fresh from the cavernous refrigerated rooms. They eat heartily, piling the meat on slabs of pumpernickel and washing it down with great gulps of dark Wurzburger which they bring in from the *brauhaus* next door.

One day as I was sitting with Ferdinand, eating a tremendous sandwich of *braunsweiger leberwurst mit speck* (liverwurst flecked with bits of fat), I remarked that it struck me as unusual to find makers of food products eating it themselves with such relish. In Fulton Fish Market, I pointed out, the mongers would rather die than eat the fish they handle all day long.

"*Ja*, that would be true of some foods," Schaller said, "but not of sausage." He speared a piece of *kolbase*, a cold pork sausage of Hungarian origin, tinged red by paprika. "With sausage, it is different. Once a man gets the taste, he never loses it. We have people come in here who have been coming in every day since we opened." He ate a piece of *kalbsrouladen* (chopped veal, pork and tongue). Then he continued, "I tell you a story about how a taste for sausage stays with a man. Years ago I had here a bologna-maker who was not a good worker. When others were busy he was wasting time. I expect a man to work for his pay. I told him, 'Work or go.' He would not work. Finally I fired him."

He paused again, surveyed the huge platter, and selected a slice of *oldenburg leberwurst* (chopped liver and pork).

"You would think," he said, "that a man I fired would be mad at me and stay mad. You would think he would go somewhere else to buy sausage. No. Today he still comes to me to buy. In fact, he is one of my best customers."

A man does not have to live near a great sausage store like Schaller and Weber in order to enjoy fine sausage. Schaller, himself, will be glad to supply a list of those he can ship, and so will Manganaro's grocery. Even mail order isn't necessary these days. The big companies—Armour, Swift, Cudahy, Stahl-Meyer—make excellent sausage which is sold throughout the country. Hormel alone makes over nineteen different dry, Italian-style sausages. Any local grocer or butcher will usually be willing to order sausage specialties. Finally, if wurst comes to wurst, it is even possible to make sausage at home. I made some not long ago and it was great. But then, I am prejudiced. I think *all* sausage is great.

But sausage-making is not necessarily fun at home. It requires strong wrists, patience, and a nose oblivious to the stinks that may arise from the pot. It is not for maidens, maiden aunts, or wives still pretending to be maidenly. It is for men, probably on a wet day, when they know the fish or deer will not be running.

How To Be Your Own Butcher

Some people like to make their own sausage from their own hogs. I don't, because I have been frightened off by Farmers' Bulletin No. 2138, of the U. S. Department of Agriculture, entitled *"Slaughtering, Cutting and Processing PORK on The Farm."* This is a pamphlet that ought to be read *after* dinner, or perhaps not read at all. It is lavishly illustrated with photographs that would make Hieronymus Bosch, if he were alive, quaver a bit. I know gangsters in Chicago who would turn their faces away from it, and a few in New York and London, as well.

12

The miniature book (it is only 48 pages long) tells you exactly what to do when you have raised a pig and want to send him to his doom. It tells about the tools that should be bought, about the block and tackle for hauling up the animal, about the care of hogs just before you slaughter them, about sticking them, about scalding and scraping, about removing internal organs, and about chilling the carcass. After that it gets into cutting the carcass, trimming pork cuts, processing, freezing, curing, dry curing, sweet-pickle curing, preparing for smoking, smokehouses, smoking cured pork, and testing smoked meat.

This is only up to Page 33. There is more pig information in here than even a pig alienist would need to know. Almost everybody but a 4-H Club boy would find it a trifle tedious, for it goes from wrapping and storing smoked meat to skipper flies, to refrigerated storage, to mold growth, to aged or Smithfield-style pork, to canning, to lard rendering, and finally, to preparing sausage. The writers must have spent a long time in Iowa and other hog states.

(Pigs make wonderful pets. Some authorities have rated them as the most intelligent of the beasts. The only problem a pet pig presents to a man living in the city is finding a suitable mudhole for him. Wives are almost never receptive to the idea.)

Back to sausage preparation.

The booklet says: "Desirable sausage can be made only from sound, high-quality materials. Shoulders, bacon strips, and even the loins and hams often are made into sausage along with the trimmings. . . ."

The book then gives us all some diagrams for (a) a barrel for smoking, (b) a frame-construction smokehouse, and (c) a cement-block one.

Presently, it gets around to the sausage itself:

You take 4 pounds of pork trimmings, 5 teaspoonfuls of salt, 4 of ground sage, 2 of ground pepper, ½ teaspoonful of ground cloves, or 1 tablespoonful of ground nutmeg. This all should be mixed together and then put through the fine blade of the grinder, and then ground through again. The sausage then should be stuffed into beef bung at once.

The Agriculture Department people now get down to business, telling us all how to make Bologna Sausage. It is no small undertaking:

You take 60 pounds of beef and 40 pounds of pork trimmings. Grind the beef in a coarse grinder and add 19 ounces of salt. Let this cool for 48 hours. The next night, add 19 ounces of salt to the pork, and grind it. Put the two together and allow to stand overnight.

Now grind the two meats together, add 1 ounce of saltpeter, 4 ounces of black pepper, 1½ ounces of coriander, and 1 ounce of mace.

Put this in a pot with 10 quarts of cold water. Mix it well. Put it through the grinder again. "Add spices . . . and mix until the mass is sticky," says the Department.

This sausage mixture should be stuffed either into bung, which I do not think is much good, or into muslin bags, which you can either buy or make yourself. It should be set aside to cool and dry overnight. Then it should be put in the smokehouse or hung over coals in the fireplace, as so many other sausages are.

"The sausage should take on a rich mahogany brown in about 2 hours' smoking," says the Dep't.

Then: "Immediately put the hot, freshly smoked sausage into water heated to 160° to 175° F., and cook it until it squeaks when the pressure of the thumb and finger on the casings is suddenly released. The usual cooking time for sausages stuffed in beef 'rounds' is 15 to 30 minutes; for larger casings, 60 to 90 minutes. Plunge the sausage into cold water to chill it. Hang it in a cool place."

Now lie down and take a nap.

You can get this book, and know how to be your own hog butcher, not to the world, but to your own family, by sending twenty cents to the Superintendent of Documents, U. S. Government Printing Office, Washington, D. C. 20402. In at least a month and a half, they will send it, in a plain, brown wrapper, if you so request.

14

No, no, here we are not talking about submarine sandwiches which are called "grinders," for some reason, in Connecticut and Massachusetts. We are talking about *meat* grinders, which no home should be without. If you are going to be a sausage cook, you must have a grinder. If you and your husband or wife do the cooking together, you probably ought to have two grinders. Grinding meat is one of mankind's true pleasures.

If you are very serious about sausage-making, you no doubt will want to invest about $43 in the Rival Grind-O-Matic, once you have stopped shuddering at its name. This is a portable electric grinder, tastefully designed. It has a little brother, a non-electric, hand-operated model, which sells for around $10.00. This is eminently serviceable.

From the Universal Chopper Division, Union Manufacturing Company of New Britain, Connecticut, you can get three separate grinders. No. 1 is the small economy size, so designated by the company. It goes for about $6. No. 2 is a bit larger. "For people with small restaurants or large families," my scout said when turning in his report. It sells for about $7. No. 3 is an enormous grinder, suitable mainly for owners of large restaurants or butcher stores. It sells for around $12.

These grinders have attachments which will enable the aspiring *wienermeister* to tuck his meat into the bung with ease. The attachments cost about $2.25 apiece, and are heartily recommended for the home *wurstmacher*. In fact, no sausage-eating home should be without one. Not all three have casing-making attachments, however. The smaller, No. 1, does not come with one.

The Enterprise Manufacturing Company of Philadelphia, makes the Enterprise Grinder. Fortunately for us all, it does not come in the shape of William Penn. It is just a simple grinder, with a detachable handle, which rests on four rubber pads on the side of your sink, table, or whatever you are using to grind on. "This looks like a good one if you have no surface to clamp a Universal to," said Dr. Hawkeye in his report. "But I think the Universals are the best. Universal is the oldest grindermaker in the country. It was founded in 1897."

Before 1897, people no doubt used ricers to make sausage. A ricer is a small but utilitarian instrument. It has a plunger with which you squeeze down soft meat, which then comes out of many hundreds of holes in its sides—or side, for a ricer is circular. This kitchen tool dates back to fifteenth-century England, I am told, but I do not believe it. I think it was invented by Tom Swift just after Mr. Damon had said, 'Bless my ricer holes!"

Anyhow, ricers can be obtained from the Rovel, not the Rival, Company, Long Island City, New York 11101, for about $2.50. I have a Rovel ricer and use it all the time. It is good for making mashed potatoes, by the way. Smashes hell out of them.

A good use to which the ricer can be put—and all the grinders, as well—is making a mess out of macaroni. The *pasta* should be cooked until it is just *al dente*, and then squeezed through the ricer and cooked in butter, or with butter on top. I have known Italian families who have fried macaroni until crisp.

Now that I remember it, there is another use to which grinders and ricers can be put. Tomatoes, onions, peppers and *fines herbes* can be put through them; also garlic, shallots, cabbage, turnips, carrots, and even watercress.

There is an old daybreak-bright saying from the uncollected works of Samuel Joseph Boal, the poet and philosopher and sometime writer, which I feel is apt to close this small chapter:

> *"What good doth a sausage-maker do*
> *Unless he doth use a grinder?"*

What good, indeed? A grinder, or a ricer, is indispensable to a sausage-maker. Choose your grinder carefully in the hardware store. Do not settle on the cheap ones. Get one you can screw on the wall so that it will always be in service—preferably one with an attachment for casings.

16

Bung or Casing

A bung may mean a stopper for a cask or keg, or a lie, or—in the words of Shakespeare—as a synonym for both a purse and the pickpocket who steals same. "To bung up," according to Webster, means "to bruise and put out of action."

In this book, bung means the casings in which sausages are stuffed. Bung means intestines of steer, veal, sheep, goat and even turkey or chicken. It especially and most often refers to pork bung, which is favored by most farmers in making sausage.

Bung should be immersed in water for about three hours. Salted water, changed every now and then. Oh, every hour or so. Sometimes it will have fatty matter in it. Some people like to leave it in, some like to scrape it out. If the beast who gave up his bung had small intestines, the latter can often be a problem, which is solved only by turning the bung inside out, being careful not to tear it in the process.

The string used to tie off bung should be the kind ordinarily used for flying kites.

Pricking—or Not Pricking—Sausage

There are always a good many arguments over sausage whenever folks of good will get together. One is whether or not to prick sausage. Another is where one will insist that the sausage made in his home county is the best on earth. Another will disagree, and the next thing will be that the two of them will be behaving like rival bourbon whiskey manufacturers, neither ever having made a sausage in his life.

"My butcher puts fennel in mine," one will say.

"*Fennel* in sausage?" the other man will say.

"Yes, *fennel in sausage.*" There is menace in the tone.

"You're nit-witted," says the second.

Within five seconds, the pair will be rolling around on the

floor, and, in the main, behaving like the climax to a Jerry Lewis film. When the fighting is all over, they will each ask the other to come and have another drink. Then they will have another fight over who gets to pay for the round.

This fight, which occurs fairly frequently among sausage-lovers, is nothing to that which occurs whenever the question comes up of *Whether or Not You Prick Sausages*. Generally, the pricking rules are these:

1. If the sausage is being started as it comes from its package or wrapping, without being steamed or par-boiled, prick it with three stabs of a fork. But turn the heat down low. The pricking releases the grease inside, which flows into the pan and imparts a nice brown-tan color to the casing and to the meat itself. This applies mainly to plain pork sausages, and to certain home-made Italian ones.

2. A hard sausage should never be pricked. For that matter, it seldom should be cooked. Hard sausage should be eaten hard and cold.

3. It is almost always the rule to prick a white veal sausage—*weisswurst, bockwurst*, et al.

4. Stomachs of pigs, goose liver sausage, and other sausages contained in various thick innards should never be pricked.

5. Tiny Viennese sausages should never be pricked. But then—they should never be eaten.

6. Some people prick frankfurters. They are wrong to do so. It just makes them wrinkle like skin that's been in a hot bath too long.

7. The huge French sausage called *saucisson* should never under any conditions be pricked. It is boiled, and the heavy casing in which it comes keeps it moist inside.

Those seven points make up the sum of what I have to say on the matter. If you do prick sausage, have a slotted spoon hard by for the skimming. Nobody loves an unskimmed boiled sausage.

ALE AND SAUSAGES. Before you get too far into this book, resign yourself to the fact that most sausage recipes are preposterously caressing to the chef's disposition and hands. Some of them may take a good deal of time, but most of them give the cook a chance to, oh, shoot some pool, play a game of chess, or even decorate a Christmas tree—or learn a new piece on the piano, or guitar or the Ungeheuer. (Where you are going to get an Ungeheuer, I cannot tell—but try.)

Get yourself some small link sausages, prick them with a fork, dump about two tablespoonfuls of butter into an iron skillet, and let them sputter and suzzle (suzzling is harder than sizzling) until they are brown and a bit crusty. Now pour on a can of Ballantine ale, or a bottle of Ballantine's India ale. Be patient while it comes to a boil, and then cover it and forget it for about a half-hour.

Cooking with them, if they are in season, I would have some poke greens, provided the poke is very young and tender. The greens should be served in a separate dish. If there is no poke, spinach will do. Or mustard greens. Or any greens you feel like serving. Or wilted lettuce, touched with garlic, come to think of it.

ANDOUILLES. I do not know how to pronounce the word properly, nor do I know its origin, but it sounds almost exactly like *ennui*. I suspect—and this is only intuitional hindsight, if there is such a thing—that it came from Provence. There is a recipe for this delicious sausage, in fact, there are two of them, in Dumas père's masterwork, *Le Grand Dictionnaire de Cuisine*. All interested in sausage are urged to try them.

To make pork *andouilles*, get some pork bung and cut it into the length you need. Soak it in a marinade of white wine, the

19

dry kind, into which you have whisked pinches of basil, thyme and two cloves of smashed or pressed garlic. Marinate about six hours. A longer time will do. Let this stand overnight, if you will.

Now. Cut strips of fresh pork, some pork fat, and some of the casings. Mix them all together with salt, *fines herbes*, and a generous amount of crushed anise with a "portar and mestle."

Remove the rest of the pork casings from the marinade and fill them with this engaging mixture. Save marinade. Go away somewhere. The idea is to let it stand for a time. When you can no longer bear the separation, go back to it, pick it up, give each tied-off link its own kiss.

Now you are ready for the drowning ceremony.

A *bouquet garni* should be lain in the reserved marinade along with one-half of a bay leaf, a little more salt, some pepper, and a hunk of pork which is approximately the size of the hunk of pork you always wish were to be found in cans of baked beans and never is. Père Dumas says you should let the *andouilles* cook in this bath and then let them cool. He is right, for I have tried it, and it is eminently palatable. Now, disagreement.

Dumas recommends that you prick. I do not. Let the un-pricked and pristine sausages brown gently in a bittering of butter, take them out, and serve them with their heat within, along with some orange marmalade.

Beef *andouilles* are done similarly. Beef bung is used, of course. Tripe and ox palates should be used, about a pound of them, well chopped or put through a grinder. Calf's udder should be added, and some ground-up bacon. These items should all be parboiled until they are just about non-resistant to the fork. Then there should be some chopped onion, cooked in butter until transparent but not golden. Four egg yolks, *fines herbes*, salt, and hard cracked pepper now go in.

Stuff the casings and tie each end with sturdy string. Boil these gentlemen in a pint of dry white wine, along with a bouquet of scallions and parsley tied together, several pieces of garlic, one-half of a bayleaf, a pinch or two of basil, three

20

or four cloves, salt, pepper, one chopped carrot and one large chopped onion. Boil them for about one hour. Take them out, drain off all the other stuff, and simmer them in a skillet in butter until they are browned and ready to eat.

Andouilles may also be made with veal substituted for beef. Various other parts of the animal may be added: heart, liver, kidneys, etc.

Andouilles should be served with home-fried potatoes, or mashed potatoes, over which the leftover butter from the pan has been poured. Along with this, serve horseradish to which beets, some vinegar, and possibly some kosher dill pickle have been added—all having first been crushed and forced through a ricer.

For some reason, no doubt hidden in my subconscious, I like to get bagels to go with *andouilles*, although there is no record in Bocca, Dumas, or any other authority that bagels are required. The sausages do not have to be simmered, by the way. They are perfectly good when eaten just out of the pot.

APPLES AND SAUSAGE. Frankly, all you good people out in cookbookland, I prefer sausage in a casing, but there are many pleasant ways to prepare uncased or loose sausage. One of them is this, which is a cinch.

Shape a pound of sausage meat into hamburger-like patties. Eight of them. Add a little dry red wine to the mixture before shaping up the cakes. Now mix one-quarter of a teaspoonful of sugar and about two tablespoonfuls of flour, and roll the sausage patties around in the mixture. Cut up four good stout apples—Winesaps, McIntoshes, Greenings, Jonathans, or any of the many varieties of winter fruit. Naturally, you will first have decored and dewormed them.

While you are cutting the apples, you should have a sugar syrup boiling on the stove; one-half cup of sugar, one cup of water, to which you will add a bit of butter roughly the size of a two-year-old's building block. Put the apples into this syrup and let them go for between ten and twelve minutes, or until they are just soft enough not to resist a poking fork.

Now put the sausage cakes on a baking-rack, or pan, or

cookie sheet, or whatever you use in your oven, and let them broil under a rather gentle flame for another ten or twelve minutes. This may also be done on an outdoor grill, in which case the sausages should be turned frequently—with a pitcher of water handy so that the grease dripping down onto the coals can be prevented from burning up everything.

The dish, whether broiled indoors or barbecued out, should be garnished with generous sprinklings of parsley, and served with Chianti, Chilean red wine, or any of the superb California wines. You eat the apples on the side. If you do the job inside, use the drippings to make a gravy and serve it over dependable mashed potatoes. This gravy should be poked up a bit with Maggi's seasoning or with some of the red wine mentioned above, salted and peppered and sprinkled with a little dry mustard. Otherwise, the sausage flavor will be overpowering and you and your guests will be depressed about the whole endeavor. This recipe will take care of four very nicely indeed.

Another apples-and-sausage dish is just as simple. Boil five or six sweet potatoes. Peel and slice them. Peel, core, and slice up five or six apples. Do not make the slices too thin.

Take a commodious casserole and coat it with oil or butter. Do not use bacon fat; if you do, you risk making the whole thing too demonstrative in asserting its porkiness. About half the sweet potato slices should go on the bottom of the bowl. Over them go four good-sized sausageburgers. And over those four lads, ladle the raw apple slices. Sprinkle all this mess gently with salt and brown sugar in about equal proportions. Now pile on the rest of the sweet potatoes, throw on a little water, and add some more brown sugar. Not too much, please. Put the casserole in the oven and bake it for about an hour and a half at around 350°. This is a good dish, but I hardly ever cook it because I don't much like sweet potatoes, except when they are baked in their khakis.

A third sausage-and-apple trick is to boil cored and peeled apples. Slice them and use these slices as the centers of sausage-burgers. These things can be broiled or fried, preferably the former, until the sausage meat is sizzlingly brown. Again, gar-

22

nish with parsley. Serve with chutney on the side, or with sour pickle relish, and trot out the mashed potatoes or French-fried parsnips.

The reverse of this is obvious. Core six or eight apples, with one apple to a guest. Leave the skins on, except for about a half-inch of naked apple around the top. Stuff each apple with either loose sausage meat or a small link, the fatter the better. Use salt and brown sugar, sprinkling all the little sentinels lightly with same. Put them in a baking pan with about a half-inch of water and lemon juice. Turn the oven to 350° and cook until a fork will penetrate the apples easily. This will be about an hour or perhaps an hour and a half. Flog onto the table the ubiquitous mashed potatoes and give each serving a liberal application of butter.

I once knew a lady who brushed these sausage-stuffed apples with honey. Too sweet for my taste, but some families have sweeter teeth than I do. If you are tired of mashed potatoes, or simply not in the mood for them, zucchini, boiled, not fried, makes a good substitute. Or, at least, an adequate one. The warning here is: do not overcook. Again, the drippings from the sausage and the water in the pan can be used to make a delicious gravy, if it is seasoned with a drop or two of Tabasco and Lea & Perrins, salted, celery-salted, peppered, and given a taste of dry mustard. Parsley, one more time, is the garnish. On the potatoes, too.

APPLE-AND-SAUSAGE CASSEROLE. This is one of the many dishes in which apples and sausages will spend many naughty prenuptial nights together.

Take as many sausages as you think you will need to keep your guests happy and satisfied. I would estimate this to be about three three-inch pork links per person. Or possibly four, if you live in a neighborhood where the old nosebag is put on regularly three times a day.

Grease a casserole, lightly. Lay down some sausages. Slice a couple of apples very thinly, the greener the better. Slice an onion very thinly. Put a layer of the sliced apples over the sausages, and a layer of the sliced onions over them. Now put in another layer of sausages, so that this orgy may come to its *Walpurgisnachtian* climax. Add one cup of water. Cover the casserole and set it into an oven and bake it all at 350° for about one hour.

Remove the cover when the hour has gone off into eternity, and thicken the whole thing with about a teaspoonful of flour and cornstarch which you have mated in a copper drinking-cup of lukewarm water. Breed them with a whisk. Pour them, in their water, into the sausage-onion-apple thing. Speak to them, or sing them a chorus of *Peoria*.

This dish, says Mrs. Ruth Luecke, its creator, is best served with hot buttered beets, and I believe her. I have no intention of telling how to make hot buttered beets; you can get that from Mrs. Irma S. Rombauer's cookbook, or from Fannie Farmer, or from *Good Housekeeping*. Oh, perhaps, I will relent. You make buttered beets by boiling them until they will take a fork through nicely, and then taking them out of their boiling-pot and skinning them. Now they are put in a very small amount of salted water along with about an eighth of a pound of butter, and allowed to heat until the butter is melted. Salt, pepper, and an almost infinitesimal pinch of thyme may be added. You need no onion with these beets. There already is some in the casserole, remember?

Some people I know like to top buttered beets with a couple of tablespoonfuls of sour cream. Some even put sweet cream into the butter-water mixture the parboiled beets are swimming in. Some have been known to add one teaspoonful of horse-radish to a pot of beets. I regard all these maneuvers as dangerously uncivilized. A beet is a beet is a beet, I say, in the manner of that grand old man Gertrude Stein, and better off not messing with it.

If beets are not to your taste, you can try boiling turnips to go along with this casserole, or even radishes. They get the same treatment as beets: boiled first, then more or less steamed with a small quantity of butter and water. Naturally, both should be peeled first; turnips, being a stored-in-the-root-cellar

24

vegetable, may take issue at being peeled and resist. Radishes should be scraped *well* beforehand and the green tops should be consigned to the garbage pail. Radishes will not put up any resistance, you will notice. In the house of my boyhood, radishes were never eaten any way but raw. It was not until I got to Provence, in my late thirties, that I learned that they could be cooked. In Montreal, some resourceful French Canadians sauté them in almost-black butter. Up there, they use tiny ones, the size of the shot that Montcalm's men must have used.

Leeks also go well with this dish, provided that they are washed thoroughly and simply steamed, having been sprinkled a bit with parsley before being plunged into their submarine graves. Braised tomatoes also can be called into service. The braiseder, the better.

Do not mix any of these vegetables with the casserole. Use them as side dishes, please, and use them carefully, gently, and restrainedly.

$\mathcal{B}$ANANAS AND SAUSAGES. Sounds outrageous. It isn't. It's delicious. Take six bananas and slit them lengthwise after having cut off the ends about one-half inch. Do not remove the skins. Force two small link sausages into the slit of each banana, and put them on a baking-sheet, or in a baking pan, or on aluminum foil, and let them go in a 375° oven for, oh, about twenty-five minutes. If the bananas aren't browned by then, let the broiler work on them for about two minutes. I would serve this with the estimable Major Grey's Chutney.

BARBECUED SAUSAGE BALLS. This recipe was printed in *The Nebraska Centennial First Ladies' Cookbook*, compiled by Maxine Morrison and edited by Catherine J. Hillegass, two ladies who ought to be called to the White House and given medals. This remarkable book, printed on the occasion of Nebraska's centennial, contains the favorite recipes of the first ladies of towns, cities, and state, and some who are first ladies only in their families.

Mrs. Dave Novotny's barbecued sausage balls are especially good, and are easy to make. About a pound of loose pork sausage should be mixed with a beaten egg, salt and pepper and approximately one-third a cup of bread crumbs.

The sausage-bread crumb-egg mixture should be shaped into balls about one-and-one-half inches in circumference, and these small spheroids then should be browned slowly in an ungreased skillet for about fifteen minutes. While they are sizzling away, you can be making a sauce of one-half cup of catsup (or do you spell it ketchup? I never know. I think it depends on what company you are loyal to). Add salt and pepper, two tablespoons of brown sugar, one of vinegar, and one of soy

26

sauce. Pour all this over the balls when they are nicely browned. Cover the spider and simmer the balls for about thirty minutes, whisking around occasionally. If you like a sauce hotter than the above, add four or five drops of McIlhenny's superb product. No other hot pepper sauce will do.

A good accompaniment for these sausage balls, would be either turnips or kohlrabi served in a separate dish. They should be stewed or steamed and buttered and salted and peppered. Serve red wine, good crusty bread, and there is a fine meal from Nebraska.

BASCOM'S STUFF. J. Bascom Wright of Knoxville, Tennessee, is a gourmet and architect of various sauces and powdered herbs which go well with sausages of all kinds. He is 61, married, has three grown daughters and two grandchildren, and, along with being devoted to his family, he has been devoted to cooking all his life.

His sauces—Bascom's Steak Sauce, Bascom's Beef Sauce, Bascom's Lamb Sauce, Bascom's Fish Sauce, Bascom's Pork Sauce, and Bascom's Picnic Sauce—are all not just good, they are great, and worth asking for at your friendly neighborhood gourmet shop.

The business, which Bascom developed when he came home from the Army in 1946, has grown to a point where it grosses around $750,000 a year and has earned a Culinary Merit Award from the New York City Gourmet Society. Bascom now makes about 260 products. "All the formulas are mine," he declares. "I developed them over long periods of time."

Unfortunately for his friends, Bascom's secret ingredients are not revealed on his sauce labels. As might be expected, the best one to use with sausage is Bascom's Pork Sauce. The label on this one says: "A table sauce for pork roast, chops, fried chicken, veal." The ingredients are listed as: "A secret blend of tomato puree, vinegar, salt, spices, soy, and 1/10 per cent of sodium benzoate."

What you do with Bascom's sauces is relatively simple. First, you try to find them. Then you try to open the bottles.

27

This is difficult. Before writing this less-than-ageless epic to Bascom, I spent nearly fifteen minutes trying to get open one of the packaged bottles he uses and I have the damaged fingers to prove it.

Now pan-boil, and then pan-fry some ordinary small link sausages. Or some loose sausage made into small patties. Do them on low heat. Wait until they are about half-done, and then put them into some vessel and set them in the oven, at about 250°.

While they're cooking, get out some of the Bascom's Picnic Sauce, and then the Bascom's Pork Sauce. Take two jiggers (two-ounce jiggers) and pour them into a saucepan. *Two jiggers of each.* Into this mixture, when it is simmering away pleasantly, chop some of the green tops of scallions, and shake in some parsley and a pinch or two of oregano. Parboil a few onions.

Take out the now pleasantly-cooked sausages and put them on some sort of a platter. Drain them first, so that they will not be too greasy. Throw a few of the parboiled onions, sliced, into the Bascom's sauce that has been simmering away. You might also put in some watercress.

Toast some corn muffins. Lay two or three sausages on each half muffin. Over this, spoon a goodly portion of the Bascom stuff that has been simmering on the stove. The sauced sausage should be garnished with more chopped scallions, or possibly some finely minced onions. Just before serving, the host should raise a glass of wine to Bascom, a noble man whose name will go down in the lexicon of great chefs.

This sausage recipe, by the way, does not have to be laid on corn muffins or corn bread. It can be put on well-toasted English muffins, or just plain bread that has been run through the toaster twice.

BOB EVANS FARMS. There are hundreds upon hundreds of small sausage producers in the United States. Among the most prominent, in terms of sales volume, is Bob Evans's, which is in a town with the unlikely name of Gallipolis, Ohio.

In 1967, Bob Evans Farms, Inc., did $9,966,198 in sales. Its new development, in 1967, was The Bob Evans Farms Sausage Pattie which is exceptionally good. The hogs who met their dooms to make these patties should be immortalized in song, story, poem, hymn, and spoken ode.

The patties can be fried, charcoal-broiled, broiled in the oven, or dumped into a pan with sauerkraut and done the usual way. They can be served on rolls like hamburgers, along with onions and pickles and mustard or ketchup. They can be broiled and trotted out with baked beans—preferably B & M—and they can be mixed up with grated water chestnuts and then steamed, thereby giving the diner a Gallipolis, Ohio, version of Chinese steamed pork and water chestnuts.

The best way I know to do these patties—I shudder whenever I write that word, so let's call them sausage cakes—is as follows:

Get one or two for each guest. Broil them on each side for about six minutes. Now take slices of sharp cheddar cheese—Swiss or even Roquefort or Bleu will do—turn the sausages and put the cheese on top.

The cheese will begin to melt soon, whether you are broiling the sausage cakes or frying them. As soon as it begins this soft and inoffensive behavior, put two slices of Mrs. Fanning's bread-and-butter pickles on the top of the cheese. Sprinkle each sausage-cheese-pickle thing with paprika. Now take some previously-grated onion and sprinkle that on rather liberally. If Uncle Rodney, the one with the bad stomach, happens to be on the premises, go easy with the onions on his.

Most guests will want two of these things. They should be served in buttered and toasted hamburger rolls after having been sprinkled lightly with dill and dried parsley and the slightest pinches of sage, oregano, and rosemary. Ketchup and/or mustard should be provided, and—for those who are not Uncle Rodney—grated horseradish.

Some nice beans should be served. Just plain beans, boiled with a little grated garlic and some parsley. To make the beans more interesting, you might break up one of the Bob Evans

29

Farms sausage cakes into them while they are cooking. Green string beans also go well with these sausageburgers and so do limas. I have known people who have used sliced dills instead of the bread-and-butter pickles.

At the side, there should be nothing but raw onions and sliced tomatoes, touched only with salt, pepper, oil and vinegar to each guest's taste. Oh, perhaps some lettuce. I hardly ever use lettuce because I hate lettuce. Another good vegetable to serve along with this simple sausageburger meal would be cold cauliflower, laved over with whatever dressing the guest might like to contrive for him or herself. Or cold asparagus. Or braised celery, served in its own dressing. Or parsnips, boiled and given forth with a nice sauce of butter. Cranberries—warm, not cold—also go happily on the side of this sandwich.

BOCKWURST. It used to be that bockwurst was obtainable only in the spring. Housewives who knew about it were always somewhat nervous when they bought it and took it home, for this sausage had the reputation of spoiling easily. The ladies thought it had to be cooked almost as soon as it was taken out of the market basket or the carryall bag, and if they allowed one bockwurst to remain in the refrigerator overnight, they threw it into the garbage or broke it up and gave it to the dog, who ate it with relish.

This is no longer the case. Today we can eat bockwurst without fear practically the whole year around, thanks to improved methods of packaging (most of which make it all but impossible to get at the wurst one is hungry for); freezing (show me a man who freezes food, and I'll show you a man who would freeze his mother); and canning. But the national demand for bockwurst has placed it in good supply throughout the country.

Nobody will tell me how to make bockwurst at home. There must be a conspiracy afoot. The undercover agents, no doubt, are handing customers leaflets saying KEEP GEHMAN FROM KNOWING. I have asked the estimable Christ Kunzler, Jr., and he has said, "Well, that's one recipe we don't give out." I have asked Ferdinand Schaller, and he has replied by showing me pictures of his three sons and himself on horseback. All the big meat packers have replied with a press release saying, "We are sorry, but we do not give out information of this kind." It does no good whatever to say, "Look, pal, I'm not thinking of going into competition with you."

Tobin's, the fine Albany, New York, firm that makes so many good sausage products, at least has the candor to put the ingredients on the label of its bockwurst. But it is a little hesitant about the proper proportions. It says that its bockwurst is composed of "Veal and pork, water, nonfat dry milk, pork fat, milk, eggs, salt, onions, spices, parsley, leeks, flavorings, monosodium glutamate."

"Spices" has me baffled. So does "flavorings." One night I caught a Lancaster butcher off his guard, and he whispered to me that "spices" meant "chives." "Ve all are gerputten der chivenhaben into der bockvurst," he said. "What else?" I asked. He clammed—or sausaged—up.

If I were trying to make bockwurst at home, I would use three-quarters of veal to one quarter of pork. The poundage would be your own choice. I would then add one egg per pound of meat, about a cupful of milk, one well-chopped leek or one smallish onion, about one tablespoonful of well-chopped parsley, a macerated clove, just enough pepper to make a skye terrier sneeze, and about a teaspoonful of monosodium glutamate. I do not know what the Tobin people refer to when they say "flavorings."

The bockwurst mixture ought to be mixed and mixed and mixed until you are so weary you are ready to forget the whole thing. It should all be ground together, smelled for the seasonings (you might want to add more chives here), and then put through the grinder one more time. At this time, you should lug out the casings you have bought at the butcher shop, soak them for a few minutes in salted water, and stuff them with the white mixture—white and green-flecked from the chives.

Tie the sausages off. They should be about the length of frankfurters. They need not be linked together. Do not smoke them. Half the fun of a bockwurst is its fresh, pungent flavor.

To cook this gentleman, boil some water until it is so furious

31

it is ready to take on the Caronia and put her on her side. Take the boiling mess off the stove, and steep the bockwurst in it after the water has calmed down. Let the villain go for seven or eight minutes. Remove the wurst with tongs, and, if you're going to eat it now, put the wurst into a frying pan that is already being made miserable by the ignominy of having butter melt on its bottom. Take that pan off the heat, too, and set it aside for a moment. Now put it back on a simmering flame and, having sprinkled the bockwurst with a cut-up raw onion, which is not really meant to be eaten, let the sausage links go until they are warmly brown all over. One or two may burst open. Be firm with them. Press them down until the insides are brown, too. I do not believe I have ever cooked a mess of bockwurst in which there was not one that did not indicate its intransigeance by splitting open and causing a general commotion in the frying pan.

Bockwurst goes well in bean dishes, especially cassoulet. It can be boiled gently, fried gently, and a cluster of it dumped into baked beans, preferably B & M. It can be eaten for breakfast with Jim Dandy grits on the side. It can be sauerkrauted, or steamed-cabbaged, or red-cabbaged. It is willing to be put on a board, cut up into inch-long slices, and served atop boiled rice, the two of them liberally rained with soy sauce, and Chinese vegetables. It can be kept, after it has been cooked and allowed to cool, and served with mustard as a kind of cold hot dog. Beef stew will not protest its presence provided it has been cut in small sections. Neither will clam chowder. Veal stew will love it, for veal is, after all, the father of this sausage.

BOLOGNA SAUSAGE. According to Mrs. Dr. S., as she is identified in *Housekeeping In Old Virginia*, there is only one method of making bologna sausage. It is one that even the most simple-minded housewife could make without difficulty. All she would need would be a pair of strong arms, for this recipe, like so many that go to make up sausage, asks for a good deal of meat.

Mrs. Dr. S.'s rules shout out for ten pounds of beef and four pounds of pork, two-thirds of the latter to be lean and one-third fat. All this should be run through the grinder, along with salt, sage, cayenne pepper, some ground black pepper, and perhaps a pinch or two of saltpeter. Choose your own casing.

There is a kind of bologna that is encased in bung and another kind that is merely wrapped in string, and yet a third kind that is done up in cheesecloth. The bung-encased and the stringed-up varieties are about two inches in diameter; the cheesecloth-enclosed kind is thick enough so that when sliced and laid on ordinary-sized slices of bread it will stick out on all four sides. This is Lebanon bologna as it is sold in the markets in Lancaster, Bucks, Berks, and Montgomery counties in Eastern Pennsylvania. But I have seen Lebanon in the Farmers' Market in Los Angeles and even in a market I visited in Denver one dismal weekend I spent there. I confess I never have seen it in Cheyenne, Wyoming, or Kathmandu, Nepal, but this may have been because I was not looking for it in those places; I had my mind on indigenous products.

Bologna originally came from Bologna, Italy. Lebanon bologna was the Pennsylvania Dutch's way of showing the Italians who was boss. The good people of Lebanon County simply refined the sausage until it was more to their local taste. It has a strong yet sweet flavor, yet it is not so sweet that it would repel a man who likes an affirmative taste in his meat. My mother used to send me off to school with bologna sandwiches so thick that if I had had the horse I wanted I could have choked him with them.

Upon the half-inch slices of bologna, she would lay slivers of either plain Lancaster County "sharp" cheese, or Amish-made Swiss cheese, and she would lave the entire thing with mustard. As I grew older, she added raw onions, or would chop up eggs that had been pickled in beet juice, or pickles she had made herself in a gigantic crock in the cellar. Even, sometimes, some sauerkraut, which she also had set in the crock herself. Not in the same crock.

One final note of advice, perhaps gratuitous: Lebanon bologna should never be cooked, unless it is to be laid over fresh

33

shad or salmon, and then it should be slivered, rinded, and sautéed gently. It should never be scrambled with eggs or heated up with poached or soft-boiled ones. It is best served as it comes—smoked, cold, and speaking its own mind.

BOYD'S SAUSAGE. I never knew Wesley R. Boyd, my maternal grandfather, who was, in order, a farmer, a breeder of trotting horses, a consumer of the crayther, and an all-around nice man, I am assured. In *buthering ceaston*, which most of his descendants spell "butchering season," he would kill his own pigs and make sausage. I daresay that pleased his progeny more than it did him, for he was more interested in his trotters than he was in the pigs.

My mother has sent me W. R. Boyd's sausage-making rule, which goes as follows:

"Grind all pork parts except ribs and hams real fine. Season well with pepper and salt. Mix for about 15 minutes. If you care to, you can grind several pounds of beef to add to this, but I never liked it that way. It's better all made of pork. If you have a sausage maker, put in a container of stuffing. Put the casing in the small pipe of the sausage maker, press the sausage in and fill up the casing. Or pack it in a pan and sell it as sausage meat."

To this, I would add some sage and some thyme, but who am I to disagree with my mother? When the old lady says "pork parts," she means the ears, the jowls, the neck meat, and almost everything else except the eyes.

BREAD-ENCASED SAUSAGE. It came to me, while I was writing this no doubt exhausting book, that sausage does not necessarily have to be in a bung or in an artificial casing. Bread will do. Provided it is Italian or French. It can even be Greek or Jewish. All it need be is long and have a good stout crust.

The McCormick people of Baltimore, one of the oldest herb-spice companies in the nation, are also of this persuasion. The recipe to follow is one of theirs.

34

Get a long loaf of French or Italian bread. Slit it in two lengthwise, at about one-third of its thickness. Set the two pieces of bread aside, first having hollowed a good deal of the bread out of the larger bottom half. You can do this with your knife or your cooking fork or your fingers. Save approximately one cup of bread for crumbing. Set aside in a dry place, or, if very fresh, dry in oven.

Now take one cup of finely minced ham and/or Spam. Do not scoff at Hormel's Spam, please. It is better than World War II GIs thought. What they called Spam is not the Spam we know today. Put the Spam or ham through your grinder with the fine blade in action. Then grate one cupful of Cheddar cheese. If you want to be daring, use Swiss.

More work is on its way. I don't know why I don't stick to simple recipes. But this really is not so labyrinthine. It only sounds that way.

Dump into a bowl one quarter cup of melted butter, the same amount of well-chopped black or green olives, two tablespoons of instant minced onions, and a quarter of a tablespoon of Colman's dry mustard. You may use well-minced fresh onion if you so desire—and I hope you so desire. Add some coarsely ground black pepper, a dash of ginger, the minced ham or Spam, and the grated cheese. Then mix it all until your wrists are ready to allow your hands to fall off.

Haul out a wooden spoon. Ladle a tiny bit of dry white wine into the bowl and mix a bit more with hands or spoon. (I assume you will have ground up cooked or smoked Virginia, Kentucky, or Tennessee hams so that trichinosis will be out of the question. There is no danger of trichinosis whatever from Spam.) When this whole bowlful is nicely muddled and seasoned to your taste, add the bread crumbs. Mix it together again. I said this was going to take some time.

Then spoon the mixture into the lower two-thirds of the loaf of bread. Now set the top part on it. Get out some foil and wrap the whole thing up, twisting the end. Use heavy duty foil, please. Get the oven up to about 350°.

This monstrous bread sausage may be helped along with the

addition of tomatoes, although they are not necessary. The ham or Spam will supply enough salt so you will not need that. The thing should be baked for about 30 minutes by which time the cheese will have melted and all the things inside will have become as close as Jerry Lewis and Dean Martin were at one time.

I serve cranberry sauce with this sausage. Or some cabbage slaw. Or some sauerkraut. It really is nothing much more than a better-than-usual submarine sandwich, but if you open the foil toward the end of the cooking, and let it get good and brown, it looks like a sausage, and may convince some people that it *is* one.

BUBBLE-AND-SQUEAK. This is a famous English dish first introduced to your respondent here by the famous British bank robber and double agent, Eddie Chapman, in a pub in Knightsbridge. We were making the traditional Sunday noontime pub crawl, and after about eleven gins apiece we felt hungry. "I know of a place where the bubble-and-squeak isn't bad by 'arf," Eddie said, and forthwith led me out to it.

The place was small. I forget its name; it was something like The Queen's Elbow. It was in a mews in a building that had been standing for at least two hundred years, slanting off to the side like its drunken customers after they left at night. There was a buzz as Chapman and I entered, for everybody recognized him. Before the war, he had been wanted by every policeman and detective in the British Isles, and had been accused of forty-odd bank robberies.

During the war, they gave him a chance to get out—provided he would attempt to parachute into France, offer his services to the Nazis, and then, pretending to act as their man, would blow up a huge industrial establishment. "Anything to blow out of stir," he said to me. "So I took the barstards up on their offers."

The war over, Chapman went completely straight, wrote a couple of books, and launched himself into the real estate business. If I had not known something of his background, I never would have believed, that day in the pub, that he once had been England's No. 1 Wanted Man.

"Try some of this, old cock," he said, handing me a dish of bubble-and-squeak. It was greenish, and looked like something the hungriest pig in the world would have turned down.

"You must be joking," I said.

"Try it," Chapman said, rather sternly. I tried it, and it turned out to be delicious. I ate two whole portions, washing it down with some Whitbread's.

When I got home, I tried to make it in my own kitchen. The effort was not successful. I could not duplicate the flavor the dish had had in The King's Truss, or whatever that pub was called.

One day some material arrived from Jones Dairy Farm. In it was a recipe for bubble-and-squeak. I had been fighting the bubble-and-squeak battle for so long I had become convinced I would never be able to master it. Tastebud memories from the Chapman lunch haunted me, however, and I decided to try the Jones rule. It turned out to be authentic, exactly as I remembered the dish at The Prince's Kidney, or whatever that tiny place was called.

Here is how it is made. Crumble one and one-half cupfuls of cold, loose, previously-fried sausage meat. While the sausage is frying, boil one head of cabbage, the dimensions of a koala bear's head. Cook it in furiously boiling water and take it out and chop it up until you get an amount that equals the sausage you are browning. Sometime during these two processes, you should be making a white sauce, seasoning it with salt and pepper, a drop or two of Tabasco, and a dash of garlic powder —but only a dash.

Put this all in a baking dish and mix it well with a wooden spoon. Cover it with bread crumbs, preferably home-made. Bake it in an oven at about 250° until the sausage bubbles and squeaks up through the crumbs. You will need no side dish for this meal. For dessert, you will want a well-ripened Brie.

Since the day Chapman introduced me to it, I have had bubble-and-squeak in many a pub in London and other English towns. It is served both hot and cold. I must say I prefer the hot. A bit of cucumber salad on the side does go well, or some raw tomatoes. Thank you, Eddie Chapman, the nicest and most hospitable bank robber I ever have known.

BUCKWHEAT CAKES AND SAUSAGES. I never much liked pancakes and I don't like the kind that are to be found in those pancake houses that have sprung up all over the country. For one thing, I cannot stand the prose that appears on their menus. Good God, even Clementine Paddleford wrote better than the people who write that copy. But I do like buckwheat cakes with sausage, and an aging relative of mine, a Miss Finetta Q. Stoneborough, once taught me to make them.

Do this the night before—just about the time Johnny Carson comes on the television. This batter, having been well-mixed with a wooden spoon during Carson's monologue, should be permitted to rise overnight.

Get two cupfuls of buckwheat flour, preferably bought from a country miller. One yeast cake should now be smashed in, and one tablespoonful of salt, plus two of brown sugar, and two cupfuls of buttermilk. Go to bed or watch TV.

In the morning, get some sausages on the stove to boil away their half-inch of water and then to sizzle in their own grease. The batter, meanwhile, has risen along with other members of the household. Take another frying pan, grease it, and drop spoonfuls of the batter in it while the sausage is frying away.

When the sausages seem to be done inside and on both sides, put them in a covered dish in the oven to keep warm. Put in a dish or a pie tin for the buckwheat cakes, too. Serve these items with gooseberry or currant jelly on the side. Some people like Vermont maple syrup, and some like old-fashioned molasses. Others have been known to eat apple butter with these cakes. Other hearty trenchermen have been known to add slices of hard red Kentucky-cured ham to the sausages. If ham is cooked along with the sausages, it should be well-minced.

After it, and the sausages, have been removed from the pan,

38

a fine gravy may be made with the addition of more of the buckwheat flour—about two tablespoonfuls, plus a drop or two of Maggi's Seasoning and one drop only of Tabasco.

CABBAGE AND SAUSAGE.   Some lady who evidently is too modest to sign her name sent me this fine recipe. The postmark said Mount Joy, Pennsylvania, and that is all I know about her whereabouts. She may be a shy minister's daughter. I like to think of her as involved with the choir director, or possibly the organist.

In the kitchen, it is plain from her prose, she is involved with good stout cooking. First she cooks one cupful of raw rice. She takes one pound of sausage, and, having drained the rice, mixes them together. While the rice and sausage are cooking in an iron skillet, she wilts a good-sized head of cabbage in hot water. Then she strips off the bigger leaves and lays them aside on paper towels so that they can drain. Next she salts and peppers the sausage and rice, and adds about two tablespoonfuls of this mixture to as many cabbage leaves as she wishes to serve. Generally, I tie this leaf-roll up with string, but it can be secured with toothpicks, which is hard on the absent-minded eater's mouth-roof.

No, she doesn't use either string or picks. "Place end down so it doesn't unravel," she says in her letter. "Unravel"? That sounds like my mother saying, "Outen the light."

Now the lady places the sausage-stuffed cabbage leaves in a large kettle, one layer after the other. She then pours in two cans of tomato paste with about a quart of water, covers it, and lets it simmer for a little over an hour.

"Good heated over," she says. And I am prepared to believe her.

CABBAGE AND SAUSAGE, NO. II.   One of the most wonderful summers I ever spent was at Pine Lake, Wisconsin. Each

40

morning, I would take my small typewriter out, along with a large envelope full of paper and carbon paper, get into a rowboat, and let myself drift in the boat to wherever the water and wind felt like carrying it and me. The boat did most of the work. I sat in it and let it bear me, and I typed on my novel.

I used to take a sandwich out on the boat, and sometimes a small thermos bottle of chilled martinis, but by the time I returned at about 6 P.M., I was ravenous. The lady who ran the house where I was staying was a cook such as I have seldom known any lady to be. When she went to her kitchen, it became a fort. I was allowed in there one day when she was busy with her stuffed cabbage. It is substantially the same, in the making, as the one given in the previous recipe, but the sauce is different. I watched her make the sausages rolled up in cabbage with awe.

First she fried loose sausage meat, sprinkling it with cumin, poppy seeds, mace, garlic salt, red pepper and black pepper, and coarsely ground salt. When she turned off the flame under the burner and drained the fat, she turned to the cabbage that she had been wilting in boiling water. This cabbage had extremely sturdy leaves and made excellent casings for the sausage, which she folded into forms about one-half the size of the average frankfurter. She folded each cabbage leaf around one of these small sausage forms and permitted me to tie each one with a length of kite string.

As I finished each little cabbage and sausage bundle, it was thrown into a frying pan that was sizzling with melted lard. The cabbage rolls were browned on both sides but not allowed to blacken.

As the sausages finished their lard bath, the lady removed them one by one and put them on paper towels to drain. She took a little grease out of the pan and threw it away, added a half-bottle of German beer to the remaining grease, plus about a tablespoonful of carroway seeds. With the remaining beer from the bottle, she made a roux with flour, and added that to the pan as well, all the time stirring as though she were bent on giving herself a crippled arm.

After the saucepan had become a receptacle for a nicely thickened but not too thick gravy, she restored the little sausage bundles. Then she quartered six tomatoes and turned them in, and dashed the mixture with rosemary and basil, stirring all the while. At the last minute the whole thing received a cut-up onion and a dash of sherry; then it was consigned to the oven. Needless to say, the skillet was an iron one.

These sausage-and-cabbage bundles can be served with mashed potatoes, but most people feel that the latter are a little much. Kohlrabi is better, if you can get it. It need only be cut up, steamed and served as it comes out of the pot. The gravy will make it taste better than it already does. It needs no butter and no salt.

CASSOULET. Eight or nine French chefs have given me their own special recipes for this marvelous casserole, and I have more or less Waringized them into one of my own.

Soak some beans—Great Northern, Maine pea beans, black-eyes, limas, and some red kidneys for color, and some chick peas (*garbanzos*) overnight. About a quarter of a pound of each kind. More, if you are expecting a good many people. Allow about an eighth of a pound of each for each person. There is much, much more to come.

Take some small link sausages—one for each expected guest, and three or four more for the pot. Sauté them gently until they are brown all around. Remove them and set them aside with tenderness. Now, take a cut-up chicken and let it cook in the sausage grease until it, too, is brown. There again, you should provide one hunk of chicken for each guest, plus a few more for the pot.

In the same dish, skillet, or whatever you are using, brown some cubed lamb-shoulder, or anything the butcher is using as customer-bait that day. Do not bone the lamb. Just cut it into good-sized cubes. Take it out when it is brown and set it aside along with its future partners in this polygamous marriage of many flavors.

Get a good-sized earthen pot, preferably one made in France.

One about eight inches deep and ten or twelve inches in diameter. Grease it with whatever is left over from that endless sautéing you have been doing. Pour the rest of the grease into the bottom of the pot.

Take the beans that have been soaking, put them into a colander and wash them, picking them over as you do.

Get a slice of pepperoni, that hard and obdurate sausage which is attributed to the Italians but which actually was invented by the Chinese who, in their Oriental modesty, would never claim credit for it. Coin the pepperoni—about an eighteen-inch slice—and have it on hand to be spread through the various layers and also put on top of the whole thing.

Now. Put a layer of beans on the bottom of the pot. Slice a tomato, a good-sized one, about as big as a ball of knitting yarn, and throw the slices atop the beans. Strew about half the lamb over the tomatoes, and cover it all with another layer of beans. (Remember to be interspersing your coins of pepperoni.) Now, in goes some of the chicken—about half, again.

More beans. Six or seven strips of bacon, each cut in half. The rest of the chicken, beans once more, and a couple of slivers of green pepper. A bay leaf. No. Half a bay leaf will be enough. The rest of the lamb and beans on top of it. This gesture ought to get rid of all the beans.

Pour in about four ounces of dry red wine, or Chianti, or, if you are pressed for supplies, sherry. Simple cooking sherry will do, but this dish tastes better if red wine is used.

Lay the sausages on top of the whole thing. Try to arrange them in the design one sees on hex signs in Lancaster County— that is, a whorled design. If there are any beans left over, put them atop the sausages.

Now slice another tomato and put it on. Lay about eight strips of bacon, cut up into two-inch lengths, all over this so that it resembles a circus big top. Spread over the whole mixture some of what I call John Cassavetes Seeds, principally because I can never remember the word carroway. Poppy seeds will do well, too.

Set the pot in an oven turned on to about 300°. Keep it at

that temperature for about one hour and then turn it back to 250°. Some people like to lay more slices of tomato on top of the topping bacon, but others feel that this makes the dish, in the argot of housewives, "too tomatoey."

While the pot is in the oven, you ought to be cutting about six slices of bread into half-inch-square cubes. Fry them in butter and permit them to stand for about three hours or until they are good and dry. Do not permit them to sit in the butter; take them out and drain them on paper towels. Set them aside. Approximately at the second hour of cooking, spread them liberally atop the dish. Add good sprinklings of salt and pepper, plus another dash of wine.

At this point, some folks I know add some poultry seasoning, as well, but I feel this is superfluous. A tiny pinch of sage or thyme, one or the other, will do. Poultry seasoning, which is composed of both, is a bit too much.

The *cassoulet* should cook all day long. It then should be taken out of the oven and be given the liberty of cooling itself. If you put it in at 9 A.M., it should cook until about 7 P.M. Then it should be set aside. It can be eaten then, but it will be far better if it is refrigerated and then eaten, heated, of course, the next day.

During the course of the reheating process, another jigger or two of wine—this time, *white*—can be added. It should be poured in carefully, so as not to make the *croutons*—the fried bread—soggy. The Thing, as I call it, because it is a taxing monster, ought to be served with a garnish of parsley or watercress.

There are those who have been known to put diced new potatoes in this mixture, adding a layer of them around the middle. In my view, it is starchy enough as it is. Potatoes are not necessary. If they *are* added, they ought to be pre-fried in the form of cubes before they are added. Some chefs add onion slices to their *cassoulet*. Others add a clove of garlic or garlic powder.

Serve this Tyrannosaurus with a very simple lettuce salad, allowing each guest to mix his own dressing at the table. Then give the people halved pears filled with about a jigger of brandy apiece. The people will leave your house dancing, making up songs to honor you, and most probably getting arrested for drunken driving.

CERVELAT. "Do you ever have sausage around the house?" I once asked my half-cousin, Tony Marshall, who was then living with his parents in Westfield, New York.

"Oh, yes, we cervelat," he said, causing his mother to give him a left hook to the left end of his mouth.

Cervelat is a thick sausage of which many Europeans and European-Americans are extremely fond. It is made with properly-prepared pork and can also be made with fish. Sometimes it is not so thick. The thickness it has depends mainly on the casings at hand.

Dumas père, in his monumental *Grand Dictionnaire de Cuisine*, offered many ways of preparing cervelat, which, in reality, is nothing much more than a rather more spiced-up version of Lebanon bologna. But, fish or meat, it is worth going to the trouble to make, if only because it will taste a bit better than the product turned out by most of the big packing houses.

To make cervelat at home, first procure about four pounds of pork and about two feet of pork bung. Clean the pork, taking out all the sinews and the fat. Put it into your grinder and add some finely chopped smoked bacon and some chopped parsley. To this add pinches of the green parts of scallions (only about one-half of a tablespoonful), a tiny bit of thyme and basil, and perhaps a macerated clove or two. Maybe some nutmeg.

All this should be stuffed unto its death in the casing, tied off in the lengths you desire, and then hung up either in the cellar or chimney for three or four days. This cervelat is cooked in beef bouillon when you finally haul it down. It is cooked for a long time—three hours, at the least—along with salt, black pepper, thyme, more basil, bay leaf, parsley and more chopped scallions. Some like to eat it hot. To my taste, it is much better when cooled.

There is a kind of cervelat they make in Lyon, France, which is delightful. They take equal quantities of lean pork, lean beef and bacon, and put all three of them together through a grinder. This is seasoned with salt to taste, coarsely ground peppercorns, shallots which have been smashed with the flat side of a cleaver, a couple of cloves of garlic which have been maltreated the same way, and a bit of saltpeter. This is supposed to be mixed thoroughly and set aside for at least two days, after which it is to be stuffed into large bungs, tied into links, and allowed to hang for about one and one-half weeks.

After the drying period, the cervelat should be hung in the chimney, assuming you have one, for another two weeks. I have the feeling that I am putting all readers off making cervelat for the rest of their lives.

Take the sausages down, pull their strings up tight, and cover them all over, rubbing hard, with a mixture of thyme, sage, and bay leaf, which previously has been boiled in white wine. Dry the sausages one more time. This will be approximately the time you will require to have a huge drunk-making drink, which you most certainly will need. Have it. When the sausages are dried again, wrap them in paper and put them away. Dumas père recommended covering them with dry ashes. I do not recommend that. For one thing, you would not have the strength.

CHEF'S SALAD WITH SAUSAGE. It ought to be made clear here that I dislike salad. Who wants to eat the stuff I fed my rabbits when I was nine? Who wants to eat something eaten by women in flowered hats? Salad, my foot.

Yet it is possible, I have found, to make a fairly passable chef's salad with sausage. Most people put bits of chicken, tongue, ham, and sometimes even veal, into a chef's salad, overlooking the delights that sausage can offer.

Pan-broil, or pan-fry, several smallish links, and when they are brown, set them into the refrigerator to cool. While the sausages are simmering, make the standard dressing: one tablespoonful of vinegar and about one-quarter cupful of olive oil. Grind some pepper into this, and add one section of finely-minced garlic. Salt it lightly, and add some Colman's mustard. Bruise everything together with the back of a spoon, then give it a whisk treatment. When you have completed that operation, place the bowl containing the dressing in the back of the refrigerator. Let it cool.

Then, put the cooled dressing into a salad bowl and tear into it shreds of iceberg lettuce, or Romaine, or endive, or chicory, or raw, well-washed spinach, or beet greens, or watercress, or cabbage, or artichoke hearts, or cold asparagus, or cold Brussels sprouts, or avocado, or thin-sliced cauliflower, or cucumber, or raw mushrooms, or olives, or some anchovy filets, or cut-up scallions, or sliced radishes, or celery cut on the bias the way the Chinese do it, or Chinese cabbage, or finnochio, or little hunks of any kind of cheese, or crumbled bits of crisp bacon, or, finally, chopped hard-boiled eggs. You can be as daring as you wish. The more daring, the better.

Take out the sausages and slice them length-wise or into one-half inch hunks. Drop them into whatever vegetables you have decided to use. Take a small slice of hard salami, about two inches of it, slice it thinly, then sliver it and put it in.

The next move depends on how hungry you are. If you wish, you can cut in slivers of other kinds of sausage or bologna, even adding some head cheese.

Now toss the salad lightly, so that each leaf gets coated with the dressing, and all the meat bits too. Set the bowl in the refrigerator, get another bowl, and muddle together two raw eggs. Set them aside for the moment. Cube three pieces of bread, melt about one tablespoonful of salted butter in a frying pan, and allow the cubes, which should be about one-half inch square, to get nearly blackened.

Remove the salad bowl again. Pour in the raw eggs, and toss the whole thing yet one more time. Take the fried bread cubes off the stove, drain them on paper or cloth towels, and add them to the salad.

Now is the time you must toss like mad. While you are tossing, sprinkle the whole thing liberally with grated Parmesan or Romano cheese or even with grated American cheese.

The experienced cook will recognize that this is not much more than a Caesar Salad made with sausage. Any kind of sausage can be used: Thuringer, blutwurst, Lebanon bologna, cooked and chilled weisswurst, cooked salami, and most of the other popular varieties.

To make this chef's salad an even more substantial repast than it already has become, a can of red or white kidney beans, which have been drained and then washed in cold water, may be added. Or *garbanzos* which have also been given the same treatment. Or both the kidneys and the *garbanzos*.

The question of what is to be eaten along with this salad is an interesting one. A variety of pickles is my choice, or chow chow, or well-pickled beets, unless you've already put some into the salad.

CHICKEN SAUSAGE HYMAN GOLDBERG. That jovial and somewhat Jovian gnome, Mr. Hyman Goldberg, who once volunteered his services to the Hearst organization as Prudence Penny, but who refused to work in women's clothes, always comes up first with a fairly repeatable joke and then with a good recipe. Goldberg, who is about as high as the average stove, attributes his success as a chef to (a) clean living, (b) total abstinence from spirituous liquors, (c) early classes in Sunday shul, and (d) his mother. His ordinary aspect, as he faces the world, is that of a man who just has emerged from bed. His eyes are blue saucers waiting to take in the day. Always nicely turned out on the streets, he spends his days insulting his friends and then goes home to Brooklyn, where he puts on the uniform of a *sous-chef* and begins to work on various cookery inventions which alarm his friends and usually delight his neighbors.

The author of *Our Man In The Kitchen* put all this into 411 recipes, each of which was preceded by a joke more terrible than the one that went before. I will spare readers the joke that preceded his recipe for chicken sausages.

Cut the meat from one and one-half pounds of cooked chicken breasts. Put it, with one-half pound of boiled ham, through the grinder, using the smallest blade. Now take one-quarter pound

48

of chicken livers, boil them in water with one-quarter teaspoon-ful of salt for five minutes, and then drain them and chop them fine. Three whisked eggs should be added to the chopped liver, plus a good-sized pinch of nutmeg, about the same amount of pepper, and one-half a tablespoonful of salt.

This all should be mixed together with the ground-up chicken and ham. Into the mixture should go three tablespoonfuls of cracker crumbs which you will have been making while the chicken livers have been boiling.

The whole thing should be put on a sheet of wax paper, or on a more-or-less greased board, and should be shaped, says Goldberg, into a roll about twelve inches long and two and one-half inches thick. Then it should be covered with more bread crumbs and dipped into three more beaten or whisked eggs. After this egg bath, it should be covered with more crumbs, treated to a second bath, and dipped again.

By this time you will be singing several choruses of *I Hate You, Hyman Goldberg*, and not even the canary will protest.

There is more to come. Get some cheesecloth, wrap the sausage-like thing in it, roll the cloth up and tie the ends with good stout string or twine.

Still more work lies ahead of you. A stock should be made from the chicken bones you have left over. About five quarts of water, plus about five tablespoonfuls of salt, all in a pot large enough to hold your sausage. When the salty chicken stock seems to be done, immerse the sausage. Cook it for at least an hour. Take it out of the stock, Goldberg advises, and let it cool for one day. Remove the cloth, he dictates. Refrigerate it overnight. Serve it on toast, cold, sliced thinly.

The sausage may be eaten hot, but it is not as good as when it is cold. There ought to be some cold cranberries on the side, whether it is eaten hot or cold. Or, perhaps, some blackberry preserves.

CHICKEN STEAMED WITH SAUSAGE. Princess Gar-den, in Hong Kong, is one of those restaurants that haunt you for days, weeks, months, and years afterward. Sometimes you awaken, 9,000 miles away, to the bleak realization that you will be able to go down the street to the local beanery for lunch and will *not* be able to get to the Princess Garden. It is not a large place, and it is decorated in a taste that might be described as Early Aw Boon Haw.

They have a dish at the Princess Garden, steamed pork and water chestnuts, that I have tried to duplicate at home many times, only to meet my usual defeat when trying to cook Chinese food. The minced pork is pressed into a flat cake, somehow, and then minced water chestnuts are forced into it. This sounds reasonably easy to do, but it is not easy at all. My pork keeps crumbling. For a while, I tried adding a beaten egg. The whole mess came out looking like Egg Foo Yung.

I have given up and have switched to another version of this delicacy, one I made up on an afternoon when I was in the United States, thinking wistfully of Princess Garden.

I got some loose sausage and about a half dozen chicken legs, and, after boiling and deboning the legs, I ground the two together. I added one beaten egg and the chopped tops of about four scallions, plus some parsley (also chopped) and some dry mustard. All this enabled me to shape it into a cake that just fits the bottom of my eight-inch iron frying pan, the one that has a lid.

I poured on water that barely covered the cake, turned the heat up high (it is difficult not to turn the heat up high when one is dealing with an electric stove, as I was), put the lid on, and sat down to have a cigarette and a drink. Then I remembered. I had forgotten to pour a little soy sauce on my simmering cake. Removing the lid, I put about ten or twelve drops of soy sauce on the cake. Then, as an afterthought, I cut up the tops of two more scallions and put them on.

Within five minutes, the kitchen was smelling the way the Princess Garden does. *More or less.* It was not quite the same, but it was a gratifying approximation. I assured myself that this was going to be one of my winners.

Ah, false courage! Ah, false pride!

I had forgotten to put in the can of water chestnuts I had opened and chopped.

50

It is advisable for anybody who wants to make this dish to attempt *not* to duplicate my omission. Steamed pork and water chestnuts somehow lose something when the water chestnuts are left out, and even the chicken does not help enough.

Later I made it again, this time not forgetting the water chestnuts, and it was even better, although I forgot to pour on, or dash on, the soy sauce. However, that item can be added at the table, as well as some more scallions, and all that is needed to go with this dish is a bowl of rice on the side, or possibly some fried noodles. Because I am wild about soy sauce, I like to make little side dishes of it with equal parts of Colman's mustard. This sauce must be used sparingly if you expect to talk an hour after it is eaten, for it is so hot it singes the tongue.

CHIPOLATA. A small Spanish sausage, differing from *chorizos* in that it is soft, not as hard as the latter. Its texture is more that of the hot dog or the old-fashioned Pennsylvania Dutch country sausage. Legend has it that the Moors brought it to Spain, which I doubt, for it mainly is made of the unclean pig. The way to serve it is as follows:

Chopped carrots, turnips, roasted and shelled chestnuts, and scallions should be cooked—without boiling—in a beef stock which has been doused with about two tablespoonfuls of sugar. If you are serving six people, you then should put in twelve *chipolatas*, and, possibly, add a glassful of water. In go four or five slices of bacon, preferably smoked. All this, when the vegetables are soft, should go into a pot with artichoke hearts, mushroom caps, and sliced, destringed, diced celery. It should be allowed to go until most of the water has cooked away. When the sauce is reasonably thick, cooked chicken or veal may be added, or kidneys, or brains, or possibly even unpickled, parboiled tripe.

The *chipolatas* may also be used as a garnish on various roasts, chops, or poultry.

CHORIZOS. *Chorizos* are a bit like Italian sausages. Some are very, very hot; others have a pleasant garlic flavor,

51

indeed a most pronounced one. Their companion sausages are called *longaniza*, which are hotter throughout. They may be obtained in most groceries that cater to the Spanish-Puerto Rican-Cuban trade.

One afternoon, I visited La Ideal Market at 166 Eighth Avenue in New York, bought some *chorizos*, and used them in a recipe I made up as I went along. Pepperoni could be used in this haphazard dish.

Chorizos are about three inches long. First I sliced them in coins of about three-eighths of an inch, put them in a skillet and let them simmer gently in the fat the heat drew from them. Then I added one onion and one green pepper, both chopped, and when the little chunks of sausage were nicely browned, I dumped in a can of El Paso Mexe-Beans. Plain kidney beans, sprinkled with dried red pepper, would do just as well. As the beans began to bubble, I sprinkled the whole thing with chili powder, black pepper, and salt, and while all those things were raising hell in the pan, I sat down and opened a bottle of Tequila I had brought from Mexico several months before.

I quartered a lime, took a pinch of salt for the tip of my tongue, bit into one lime quarter, and tossed off the Tequila. Soon the aromas rising from the chorizos and beans were more than I could bear, so I called a friend of mine, told him to get over to my place as fast as he could, and to get a loaf of French bread on the way. He brought not just bread, but Chianti, plus some black olives.

We had a few more Tequilas, toasting everyone Spanish we could think of except Franco. We opened the wine. The stove continued to send up inflaming odors, and I wished we had had a couple of sombreros to wear. Presently we began to play pool. This was a mistake, for in the middle of the second go at nine-ball, the stuff on the stove began to burn. I ignored it, thinking that some of the beans were just sticking to the bottom of the pot. I was wrong. Oh, how wrong I was. We had to go out and get some hamburgers.

A couple of weeks later I tried my chili again. This time it was fine, for by then the Tequila was all gone.

CORN AND SAUSAGE STUFFING FOR POULTRY. There are so many ways to do a stuffing for poultry, it seems gratuitous of me to hand one out. This one is especially good, I think, and ought to be shared.

Two boxes of frozen corn, or the equivalent of fresh, or two cupfuls of John Cope's dried corn, are cooked and then drained. About a pound of loose sausage is cooked until brown but not crusty. Take out the sausage and leave some of the drippings in the skillet—about one-quarter cupful. Add one cupful of chopped onion and cook until golden. Now, add the cooked corn and the sausage, and mix everything together with a wooden spoon, adding salt, pepper, and one and a quarter teaspoonfuls of poultry seasoning. This ought to make enough to stuff a 14-to-18-pound turkey.

A sausage stuffing without corn, but with bread crumbs, can also be made, using roughly the same rule. I know one lady who, to my delight, used lima beans instead of corn. Another used chunks of hominy grits, and yet another put hunks of pineapple in with the meat mixture.

A note of caution: Italian and Chinese sausage do not go very well as stuffing material unless the bird is a duck. And then you have the grease problem.

COUNTRY SAUSAGES AS MADE BY MRS. JOHN M. MOORE. As I quickly learned when I began my blundering inquiries into sausage-making, there are more ways to do it than I ever had imagined. Sausage-makers seldom agree on what to put in. For example, Christ Kunzler probably would not agree with Ferdinand Schaller, and it is probable that neither of them would agree with sausage-makers in Cincinnati or Phoenix or Chicago.

The home recipes are the best for the home cooks, and I have one here in a letter sent along by Mrs. John M. Moore of Lancaster.

Mrs. Moore says: "Take six pounds of lean fresh pork, three pounds of chine fat . . ." and there she lost me. What *is* "chine" fat? I wondered, and forthwith looked it up, to find that it is fat around animals' backbones.

To the pork and chine (sounds like an old-time vaudeville duo), add three tablespoonfuls of salt, two of black pepper, four of pounded and sifted sage (you can use powdered), and two of summer savory. The meat should be chopped finely or ground, along with the seasonings.

"Mix it with your hands. Taste it to see if it has the right flavor." I think that's risking a disease my mother used to call "trichiny," which was her family's Safe Harbor way of pronouncing "trichinosis." Instead of tasting, I would smell it.

Next comes Operation Bung or Bag. "Each bung or cheesecloth bag should be filled with enough sausage to make one family dish," says Mrs. Moore. The bungs or bags should then be dipped in melted *lard* and put on hooks or nails in a cool, dry place.

Mrs. Moore says, "Some prefer to pack the meat in jars, pouring melted lard over it, to be taken out with the hands as wanted and moulded into small patties. Many like other spices added—cloves, mace and nutmeg." I would go easy on these additives, putting in only pinches of same.

If you have one of those small smokehouses, available for about forty dollars from such New York stores as Abercrombie and Fitch or Hammacher Schlemmer, or possibly even from your local hardware store, you might try smoking some of your bung- or cheesecloth-encased sausages. They will last longer if you smoke them.

If you haven't got a tiny smokehouse tool, you can build a fire in the outdoor barbecue and stand by with a bucket of water, dousing the coals liberally to send smoke up to the sausages on the grill. After each dousing, the coals will quickly revive, and the smell may send you dancing all over the lawn, singing every last verse and chorus of Shall We Gather at the River? or possibly, This Is Your Last Chance, Clancy. Men should wear derbies during this ceremony, and there should be liberal quantities of malmsey or mead.

Once Mrs. Moore has made her sausages, she cooks them in

a manner that brings out their true flavor. She puts a small piece of lard or butter into a large skillet. By "small piece" I believe she means about a tablespoonful-and-a-half. Lard is better, if you can *find* lard, which has become increasingly difficult in these addlepated years.

We come now to the eternal do-you-prick-or-don't-you? question. Mrs. Moore advises pricking with fork, or, if you can find one, ice pick. "Lay the sausages in the melted grease, keep moving them about, turning them frequently to prevent bursting. In ten or twelve minutes they will be sufficiently browned and cooked."

This is not enough time, in my opinion.

"Another sure way to prevent the cases from bursting is to cover them with cold water and let it come to the boiling point. Pour off the water and fry them. Sausages also can be nicely cooked by putting them in a baking-pan and browning them in the oven, turning them once or twice." For this process, I would recommend heat of about 300°. "In this way you will avoid all smoke and disagreeable odor. A pound will cook brown in ten minutes in a hot oven," says Mrs. Moore.

Sausages done this simple way are best served with grits (Jim Dandy—what other kind?) and some scrambled eggs done in the sausage grease. They should be accompanied by a slice or two of tomato—very thin slices—and perhaps some onion—also sliced very thin. There should be toast so burdened by butter that it looks as though it might come apart, and there ought to be some fine English marmalade to accompany the toast. Some people might like to fry slivers of Kentucky ham, or Smithfield ham, or any dried and cured smoked ham, in a separate pan alongside the sausages. Some might want to supplement the sausage with strips of smoked bacon, preferably the product of Jordan's Old Virginia Smoke House, established at Smithfield, Virginia, in 1840.

I thank you, Mrs. John M. Moore.

CRANBERRY-SAUSAGE CASSEROLE. There was an old Bob and Ray radio routine in which Bob, playing the part of

Wally Ballew, "the winner of many television and radio awards," interviewed a Cape Cod cranberry farmer.

The farmer was surprised to learn that cranberries could be used in cranberry sauce, cranberry juice, and other ways. Ray, playing the farmer, said: "To tell the truth, cranberries don't move very fast. People don't seem to like them." And, farmer-Ray added: "I've got to write all this down. Cranberry juice, you say? Tell me, are there two i's in juice?"

The "farmer" would probably have been amused to learn that there is a wonderful dish that can be made with cranberries and sausage.

Wash and pick over, or cull, two cups of fresh cranberries. Turn the oven to 350°. Put the cranberries, and about one cup of granulated brown sugar into a commodious casserole. Stir the sugar and the cranberries until they are so close that if they were human, they would feel like exchanging Shrine fezzes.

Boil for a bit, but not long, four or five sweet potatoes. Peel and slice them. Add about a half-cup of water to the cranberry-brown sugar mixture, and put the sweet potato slices over the berries. Now, take about, oh, a dozen links and put them on top. Salt and pepper them liberally.

Italian sausages may be substituted for fresh or smoked pork links. The casserole should be baked for about one and one-half hours, after which the cover should be removed and the whole thing should be allowed to go in the oven until the sausages are brown all over. Turn them occasionally, if you wish, trying not to prick them. Use a wooden spoon.

The casserole is good all by itself, but it can be improved by the serving of fresh peas or corn on the side, along with some coleslaw or some of Fanning's delightful bread-and-butter pickles. Along with it should go some crusty French or Italian bread, so you can mop up either while you are eating or afterward. The bread should be fresh, and never, under any conditions, toasted.

Wear a NEW YORK TIMES apron while doing this dish. It is a ripe green, approximately the color of those apples that used to give little boys stomach cramps, and may be obtained

56

at this writing at a cost of about $2 from Nat Goldstein, Promotion Manager, New York Times, Times Square, New York. If you invite Goldstein over to your house to sample your casserole, you may get one free.

CREAMED POTATOES AND SAUSAGE. Mrs. Diane Shiflet, of Bareville, Pennsylvania, is not a friend of mine, but I hope she will be one day.

She takes a pound of sausage, either loose or cut out of the casings, or cut in one-half-inch pieces, while still in the casings, chops an onion fine, and fries the sausage and onion together until the sausage is slightly brown. I do not know what she means by "slightly" brown, but I suppose most housewives will understand that. Set aside about two tablespoonfuls of the sausage grease for later use. She now adds water to cover the sausage and onions forgets them for ten minutes, having first turned down the heat a bit.

While the sausage and onion are bubbling along together, Mrs. Shiflet takes four or five potatoes, cuts them in quarters, and adds the pieces to the sausage and onion, salting and peppering in approximately the following proportion: one and one-quarter teaspoonful of salt and one-quarter teaspoonful of pepper. She covers her skillet and lets the whole glorious mess cook until the potatoes will just about break apart at the touch of a fork. This is kind of a boiled hash.

No, it is not. It is a little more complicated than that.

A roux now must be made, consisting of one cup of gently-warmed milk and two tablespoonfuls of flour. This should be added to the sausage-and-potato bits and cooked until it is thickened.

"Parsley may be added to the mixture to add color," Mrs. Shiflet wrote me. They—fresh parsley sprigs or parsley flakes—also add some flavor, I maintain.

CUCKOLDS. For this recipe, the late Gerald Kersh used three ounces of suet, one onion, eight ounces of venison, three ounces of oatmeal, and salt and pepper.

Before blending the above ingredients, Kersh would take a number of venison tripe skins, meaning the stomachs of deer. "Wash the tripe skins and turn inside out," he wrote. "Do not remove the fat on the inside. Mix together the venison, which you will have chopped finely, the suet, also chopped, the oatmeal, salt, and pepper. Fill the skins loosely with this mixture and prick the skins. Tie them at both ends. Boil for about forty-five minutes. When wanted for use, fry them in a little hot fat until browned or grill them for fifteen minutes. Should be served hot."

DUTCH SAUSAGE WITH GRAVY.

For Dutch sausage, the cook must first take at least one pound of loose pork sausage. This loose meat is fried in however much Crisco, or ham fat, or bacon fat, or even oil of some kind, as the cook thinks it needs to get brown.

The rest of this is so simple that it could be done by an escaped convict hiding out in a mountain cabin, Humphrey Bogart style, provided he had brought along the ingredients. When the sausage is brown, it should be removed from the pan and set in an oven-proof dish of some kind, and put into a 350° oven. At the same time, put in one split English muffin for each guest.

Work swiftly, now. Pour half the grease away from the sausage pan. Use enough flour to make a roux with the remaining grease. While you are whisking that roux, add equal parts of water and milk, very gradually. Pour in one capful of Kitchen Bouquet, and whisk that around. By now the English muffins will be toasted. Spoon about two tablespoonfuls of sausage on each English muffin half and pour over it some of the thickened gravy, approximately one teaspoonful of sausage, some monosodium glutamate, and perhaps some garlic salt, plus, of course, salt and pepper and a bit of celery salt.

If you are serving this for breakfast, put some kind of potatoes on the side. Home-fried or raw-fried, preferably. If you are doing it for lunch, raw cucumbers and tomatoes with an oil and vinegar dressing. If it is for dinner, serve the cucumbers and tomatoes and add a baked potato with plenty of butter on the top. Or set out some lima beans, fresh or frozen, or some Cope's corn.

Alongside should go some Pennsylvania Dutch coleslaw,

which is made by chopping green peppers and cabbage until the bits are about one quarter of an inch square, and then immersing them in about one cupful of white vinegar, one-half cupful of water, 2 teaspoonfuls of sugar, and about one-half teaspoonful of salt. Pepper it if you wish. It doesn't really need it.

DUTCHMAN'S STEW.   A good many of the recipes in this book came to me after I wrote a letter to the newspapers in Lancaster, Pennsylvania, asking for new or old, interesting or unusual ways of preparing sausage. Mrs. Mildred M. Bahn gave me this one.

Mrs. Bahn takes 1 pound of smoked link sausage and 3 medium-sized potatoes, pared and cut into quarters. She then gets a good-sized head of cabbage, cores it, and cuts it into what she calls "small wedges."

In a pot, she brings 3 cupfuls of water to a treacherous boil, meanwhile cutting her sausage links into two-inch pieces. The sausage is put in when the water is boiling like crazy, and then the potatoes and cabbage are added.

After that, she turns down the heat and simmers this whole delicious concoction for between 15 and 20 minutes, or until the potatoes and cabbage are tender. It should be lightly salted and peppered, I can attest, for I tried it one night without using salt and pepper, and the arm movements of my guests made them all look like a convention of weight-lifters.

Stewed tomatoes go well on the side of this stew, or Cope's corn, or steamed cauliflower.

Eggs and Sausages

EGGS AND SAUSAGES. There is no trick to this dish. There are two rules to follow:

1. You do sausages in a skillet or, if you wish, a spider, until they are nicely browned, pricking them or not pricking them, as you wish.

2. You make some eggs—sunnyside up, over easy, scrambled, whatever way you like.

With toast or an English muffin on the side, and possibly a garnish of watercress and a side dish of home-fried potatoes, this makes as enjoyable a breakfast as any person possibly could want. A little orange marmalade on the side, perhaps, but only a little.

There are variations. Sausages can be broiled until they are dark, dark brown and then put through your grinder, skins and all, with a medium sized onion or two, and then strewn into eggs, which you already have beaten with a whisk. The eggs should have two tablespoonfuls of water for each two eggs. Also, a pinch of parsley such as a two-months-old baby might be able to get between his thumb and forefinger.

If you are fortunate enough to get to England, buy an egg coddler for each and every member of your family. Buy the two-egg size. Broil or fry some sausages, drain them, chop them into coins, and go as follows: two or three coins on the bottom of the coddler, one egg broken over that, some more coins, another egg broken, and a few sausages on the top. Screw the lids of the coddlers on as tight as you can get them, and drop them gently into water that is boiling as though it were the sea that put Ulysses and his men amongst Miss Circe and her ladies. About four minutes of immersion should do. Take the whole mess out of the coddlers and serve each portion on dry toast. Dash with Tabasco, but only a drop or two.

A man I know, Elwood P. Fenstermacher (as God is my Judge, that is his name), bought an egg-poacher in a store near Wheelwright, Ohio. One morning, while poaching eggs in this pan, he dropped a small piece of sausage into each one, dotted it with salt and pepper, and pronounced the resulting egg dish superb. Fenstermacher may have been carried away by the pride of his new possession, but I have tried out this recipe and it *is* superb.

Sometimes eggs are improved by being basted with sausage grease. But, most often, it is better to cook the sausages separately and then pour a little grease on the eggs later. No cooks ever agree about this matter.

ELLA'S SAUSAGE AND NOODLE DISH. Two close, old, dear friends of mine are Ella Fraunfelter and her son, Robert, who live together in Lancaster, where the farm markets have taught them how to live extremely well. Fraunfelter, at this moment in history, must weigh at least 598 pounds. He is always shaking his head over his girth. He, himself, does not much mind the crane he must hire to get him into his car in the mornings, but it makes an obscene racket in the neighborhood. Dogs bark at it, and the neighbors sometimes send him notes containing pure irritation.

Here I have been exaggerating. Fraunfelter only weighs about 453 pounds. He attributes his modest, sylphlike frame to good habits and the cooking of his mother.

Ella and Robert Fraunfelter eat well, not to say frequently, except on Friday and Saturday nights, when Ella repairs to some local shebeen, and, after some hoisting of the Gambrinian (as Col. John R. Stingo used to call it), cocks her hat on the side of her pretty head and sings a chorus or two of *I'll Be Glad When You're Dead, You Rascal You*. This generally is followed with a touching rendition of *Jesus Wants Me for a Sunbeam*, during which one of her friends does a remarkable imitation of a pipe organ in the background.

62

During the weekdays, Ella is remarkably, or at least notice-ably, restrained. She is a first-rate cook, and one of the things she makes for the behemoth she has spawned is a sausage and noodle dish.

Ella takes one pound of loose sausage meat and browns it in a pan with a chopped onion that previously had been the size of her son's ears bunched together. She drains off the excess fat, adds about six ounces of uncooked noodles or macaroni, plus two cans of tomato paste and two cupfuls of water. "Cover and cook slowly about twenty-five minutes," she admonishes. "Bob and I like this dish very much. It is real tasty and very filling. With it, I serve Harvard beets and a tossed salad and apple pie for dessert."

Ella does not mention the herbs that go into this creation of hers. I would think a small pinch of oregano, a very small sliver of bay leaf, and the usual salt and pepper, along with a dash or two of monosodium glutamate. All that is up to the cook. If the cook happens to be Ella, the whole thing will turn out to be just fine, except on Fridays and Saturdays.

ESCAROLE SAUSAGE. It sounds ridiculous. Go ahead and let it sound ridiculous to you. The fact remains, there is a sausage that can be made with a casing of escarole, and a de-licious one at that.

Take three-quarters of a pound of sweet Italian sausage and one-half pound of hot. Decase it, and brown it gently in some olive oil. I don't know how much. This was fairly greasy sau-sage, so I didn't need much. If you can't get Italian sausage, ground chuck will do, by the way.

Next, I put together, in a pot, two heads of escarole, first tearing off the bad leaves of this member of the chicory family. I blanch these heads. Then, drain the water from the pot, put on a pair of gloves and tear the largest leaves off the two heads.

Now I go back to the sausage that has been simmering, and add to it one can of flat-out anchovies, a crushed clove of garlic, enough parsley to choke a rabbit, about one cupful pitted black and green olives, one-half cupful bread crumbs, and two tablespoonfuls of *pignola* (pine nuts). Salt and pepper also goes in, and I always add oregano.

An old Italian chef taught me how to do this. How furiously he stirred it! Toscanini himself never used his hands with such furious grace. This gentleman, a certain Mario Ferrari, worked in a restaurant in the Mulberry Street section of New York City, cursing all the while. His help did not like him much, for he was always brandishing knives. I liked him because he taught me so much of the little I know about cooking.

"Looka here," Mario would say, ripping the biggest leaves off the escarole. "You do thisa." He laid two leaves side by side, overlapping one over the other by an inch and a half.

Mario took some of the sausage mixture and folded the escarole leaves over it, making a neat little sausage. He then tied this with string, wrapping it around the leaves, first horizontally and then vertically. He put a little more oil on each of the little sausages he made and put them all in a skillet along with some beef stock, covered it, and simmered it for about one-half an hour.

"You gotta add some more watta if you want it to be done nice," Mario said.

This serves as many people as you want it to. Make two per person. It's one hell of a chore to tie up all those leaves, but it's worth it. The Italian name for this dish is *Escarola Imbottita*. It should be served with Chianti, and perhaps some currant jelly. No coleslaw, please. The casing of this small sausage serves well for the greens. You can, if you wish, serve some steamed lima beans with it, or some corn.

FERHOODLED SAUSAGE. I do not know Mrs. J. Henry Herr, of 2064 New Holland Pike, Lancaster, Pennsylvania, but I wish I did. At least I wish I could get to call her up some time when I am in Lancaster and say something like "Say, Mrs. Herr, when are you going to make some ferhoodled sausages and invite me out to your house?"

It should be explained to all those who do not live in the area of true civilization, the Pennsylvania Dutch country, that "ferhoodled" means "all mixed up," or, sometimes, "demented." Mrs. Herr's sausage recipe is ferhoodled, all right, but it is not that of a demented lady. It comes from a cook who knows exactly what she is doing.

It requires about one-and-one-half pounds of loose sausage which must first be crumbled and browned in a skillet. After it is browned, the fat should be poured off and the heat turned down. Add one large chopped pepper, two or three celery stalks, destringed and chopped, one cup of uncooked rice (not the instant kind), two chopped scallions and one cup of cold water to the meat. Turn this down to low heat, ladies, and go to your crewel work for at least half an hour. Then add to the sausage one tablespoonful of Lea & Perrins and salt to taste. Get back to your crewel work, or your silver polishing, or whatever it is you are doing, for a final thirty minutes.

It strikes me that carrots cooked first in butter and allowed to get politely, not demonstratively, brown would go well with this. I have an old carrot trick I do with the skill of a Harry Blackstone. After the carrots are just about done in their bath of melted butter, I pour a shot of bourbon or brandy. I do not pour this into my stomach. Instead, I put it on the carrots, sprinkle them with sugar, and set fire to them with an old-fashioned match. The brandy flame goes practically to the ceiling. The bourbon does not go quite as high, but if this stunt is performed, it is provident to remove all the nylon or organza or cotton net curtains in the kitchen, or else invite the local fire chief for dinner.

Cold cucumbers, chopped in thin slices, laid on a plate alternated with quite thin onion slices, go well with this, too, as long as they are covered with a fairly mild dressing composed of nothing but olive oil and a mild vinegar. At the end, a French or Danish Brie. With it all, either beer or a good cheap red wine, Italian or domestic.

If you invite me, Mrs. J. Henry Herr, I'll bring the wine. I may even bring you a new crewel needle.

FRANKFURTERS, OR THE NOBLE HOT DOG.   The history of the noble hot dog—that is, it is noble if it is prepared and served properly—is clouded with confusion and contradictions. It is generally agreed that this sausage originated in the city that gave it the name, Frankfurt-am-Main, Germany. Nobody can say with certainty who invented it. The American Meat Institute says it was introduced into the United States by a Bavarian peddler in St. Louis, Missouri, named Anton Ludwig Feuchtwanger, around 1876. This enterprising gentleman had been handing his customers gloves to handle his hot sausages without burning their fingers, and one day, according to the Institute line, he hit upon the idea of wrapping his frankfurters in buns. Actually, frankfurters in buns were being sold in New York City as early as 1871. The AMI story is a lot of bologna.

Another AMI story says that purveyors at the Chicago Columbian Exposition of 1893 established the frankfurter, which I also doubt, because Usinger's of Milwaukee, Wisconsin, were making them back as far as 1870. It is doubtful if the origins ever have been traced successfully.

On the other hand, who cares? The hot dog is America's favorite food. We eat about eight billion of these *wurst* per year. The expression "hot dog!" has become synonymous with enthusiasm, not only here, but in England, France, Germany and Italy.

66

T. A. Dorgan, the newspaper cartoonist, is generally credited with coining the phrase. Originally, frankfurters were called "Dachshund sausages "because of their shape—roughly that of the beloved badger hound. Dorgan used to draw little frankfurters walking about, playing tricks on each other, commenting on politics and social customs, fashions, morals, etc.

It is most likely that Charles Feltman, the Coney Island butcher credited with making the first all-beef frankfurter, and his imitators out there, were responsible for the frankfurter becoming known as the Coney Island Red Hot. These delicious items are sold under that name everywhere in the country. Nathan's, of Coney Island, has established a frankfurter reputation that is worldwide. Nathan's sells about a million pounds a year.

Nobody from Nathan's, not even a defector who has moved into the city, will give out the recipe for the Red Hot Sauce. It consists of ketchup, Tabasco, onion juice, mustard, pepper and salt, with some powdered cloves and nutmeg, both in pinches, and some sprigs of parsley which will disintegrate as the sauce simmers—and it should simmer for around two hours.

Instead of ketchup, I like to use a combination of half fresh tomatoes and half ketchup. I use more Tabasco than probably is necessary. I like onions with my hot dogs, chopped until they are about the size of large diamonds. Sometimes I like sauerkraut, sometimes not. It depends upon the day and the condition of my stomach.

The frankfurter is indeed a noble beast, measuring about five and one-half inches long by about three-quarters of an inch in diameter, unless you are talking about the king-sized ones, which are twelve inches long and made by men who are interested more in novelties than in food.

The standard one usually has 4.5 grams of proteins, large quantities of vitamin B and iron, and carries only around 140 calories. According to the label of the Tobin Company of Albany, New York, in addition to beef and pork, it is composed of pork fat, water, corn syrup, salt, dextrose, spices (the company does not say *which* spices), flavorings (the company does not say *what* flavorings), monosodium glutamate, sodium ery-thorbate, and the sodiums nitrate and nitrite. This Tobin frank-furter, called "frankfurt" by its mother company, is as good as those of Usinger's and Kunzler's and Schaller und Weber's, and it can be ordered from Tobin because it is INSPECTED AND PASSED by the U.S. Dept. of Agriculture, and Tobin therefore can send it through the U.S. mail.

Frankfurters are usually made by combining sixty per cent beef and forty per cent pork, although fifty years ago the pro-portion was the other way around. Kosher hot dogs are all beef and, to my taste, are terrible. Most hot dogs are seasoned with crushed garlic and a number of herbs which no sensible sau-sage maker will reveal. There are three great places in the United States to buy them: Usinger's in Milwaukee, Schaller und Weber in New York, and Kunzler's in Lancaster.

I understand that there are good frankfurter shops in St. Louis, but I never have gone hunting for them in that city. Some restaurants of the soiled-fork persuasion keep them sim-mering constantly on the grills, but it is my view that, unless they are skinless, which tends to make them taste less good than the bung-encased ones, they should *not* be grilled. The outside of a frankfurter ought to be so soft it can be cut with a fork or with the teeth.

Indeed, there is only one way to do a frankfurter properly. Boil about one quart of water. When it is boiling like the sea that wrecked the *Hesperus*, throw in about one tablespoonful of salt, and take the pot off the stove if you have an electric one—and if you do, you and I hereby part company. If you have a logical, functional gas stove, simply turn down the flame. Take out six or eight frankfurters. Do not toast the buns, unless you have had them around for three or four days, in which case you probably ought to split them, butter them, and place them for a minute or two under the broiler, crust side down.

When the boiling salted water has calmed, the frankfurters should be added and the pan covered. They should be permitted to remain submerged for no more than seven minutes, and then they should be removed, snuggled into a towel, paper or cloth, to dry them, and placed instantly on their buns, served on paper plates, surrounded by stuffed green and plain black olives, Fanning's bread and butter pickles, slivers of Kosher pickles, dabs of mustard and ketchup, and sprigs of parsley. A large bowl of chopped onions should be placed at hand. Some people like sweet relish; they are barbarians. There should be paper napkins beyond the dreams of the manufacturer's avarice, or paper towels, or bathroom paper. For very small children, there should be enormous bibs, and the hot dogs should be cut in thirds.

Some people serve side dishes, such as canned baked beans, on the paper plates beside the frankfurters. Baked beans are fine, but only if they are those put up by B&M. Some of the other brands do not seem as satisfactory as they did to me in my boyhood.

Before offering a series of frankfurter recipes, a sausage sometimes called "wienies," "wieners" or "weenies," let me offer a few tips:

1. Never buy canned frankfurters if you can help it.

2. Always try to get fresh ones from a *German* butcher.

3. Do not buy them at a ball park if the man selling them wears a moustache.

4. Do not fly to Milwaukee to buy them at Usinger's, for the chances are that if you arrive there after noon, that superb shop will have sold out its supply by 11 A.M.

Now for variations on the hot dog theme.

The simplest way is to cut frankfurters in about two-inch lengths, douse them briefly in the previously-boiled water, and then open a can of beans and let them both get hot together. Fresh raw onion, chopped or cut into rings, may be put on top just before serving. A few springs of parsley and a tiny pinch of oregano.

This dish can be enhanced by fresh or smoked pork links, previously browned or parboiled, and cut the same size as the frankfurter sausages. I would add some more ketchup, and possibly a dash or two of vermouth. A wild friend of mine once poured in some bourbon. It was not much good, except to him, but then, he was from Louisville. Red wine is fine, but only a dash.

Cut-up frankfurters can be added to pea soup with good results. Beforehand, fry some croutons, but they should be put in only after the frankfurters have been steeping for a while. Then the croutons can be sprinkled across the top of the pea soup. This must be done at the last half-minute before serving; otherwise, the bits of bread will get soggy.

Need I mention that a splendid dish can be made with frankfurters and sauerkraut? All that is needed is one-half a handful of carroway seeds, a cut-up and cored apple, and an onion. Some add white wine to this. I have known cooks who have added red wine, and I have made it a point to avoid their tables. The wine must be white, dry, and harmless, and there must not be too much of it.

Pigs in blankets, frankfurters that have been encased in dough and baked, are favored only by women who got their cooking instructions from magazines edited by people who know less about cooking than I know about the Stanley Steamer.

The recipe for them is not hard. You take a frankfurter and wrap it in Bisquick dough and put it in the oven. Then set that oven for about 350° and try to forget the whole thing. Kids like this stuff sometimes, but not often.

It can be improved slightly, if the pigs in their dough blankets are brushed with butter and sprinkled with parsley. But not much improved. This recipe was invented by some frantic lady dietician working for one of the meat companies, a big packager, who insisted that she come up with something new if she wished to hang onto her job. Melted cheese poured over it will not help it. Neither will the Red Hot sauce mentioned before. If you want to keep whatever reputation you have as a cook, you will never serve it except to children.

Frankfurters may be placed in split Shredded Wheat biscuits, after they first have been browned in a skillet and the Shredded Wheat pillows have been toasted in the oven. Two

70

of the wieners to each split hunk of biscuit. The tops should be served with butter and put on the table with maple syrup or molasses. A good breakfast dish. I serve home-fried potatoes on the side.

Another baked dish for which this most serviceable *wurst* may be called up involves gashing them lengthwise with a knife and filling the slit with mashed potatoes. This is topped with some crumbled or grated cheese and a sprinkling of onions. It is baked in an oven that has achieved a climax of about 400°. It is fine for lunch, especially if you happen to be not especially hungry but need something sustaining.

Frankfurters are sometimes used in poultry stuffing. The housewife coins them and adds the coins to her ordinary stuffing, which is, according to her family's taste, enhanced by them. Other cooks I have known have sliced them lengthwise and filled them with the standard poultry stuffing, then baked them. Not a great tantalizer. One night I opened a can of lima beans and sliced some frankfurters into the stewpot, added some onion and salt and pepper and a sprinkle of sage, and the thing came out surprisingly good.

Apples go well with the complaisant hot dog, especially if they are first browned in butter, chopped a bit, and then richocheted into the steaming frankfurter bath. This must be done with a certain deftness that only the experienced chef can summon.

Strangely enough, even Southerners eat hot dogs from time to time, but in my view they do them oddly.

They take an onion, a half-cupful of sliced or chopped pepper, and an equal amount of cut-up celery which has been destringed, and they sauté all that together. To this is added eight or nine frankfurters—two per person—cut up in rather generous pieces, about two inches long. Then, in go two-and-one-half to three cups of canned or fresh tomatoes. The tomatoes and frankfurters are dusted—only dusted—with oregano and thyme, and everything is simmered in the pan for about ten minutes, after which it is put in a casserole and let go for a little while. Now a piecrust topping, made of corn bread from

Jim Dandy, is put on the top of it, and the whole thing is baked until this topping is brown. This takes between twenty and thirty minutes.

Another recipe that can be done with corn meal involves making a package of the Jim Dandy kind without following the directions on the label, which call for a cup of corn meal and a cup of water.

A better recipe is to take two cups of milk and a cup of Jim Dandy in a double boiler, stirring as long as your arm can survive. This fatiguing process should go on for nearly half an hour. Now, add one tablespoonful of butter, three-quarters of a cup of grated cheddar or Gouda, and keep churning with your wooden spoon until the cheese has vanished into the whole thing. While you are spraining your arm, be cutting the frankfurters in half lengthwise, one or two for each person you are planning to serve.

Two eggs should now be hauled out of the refrigerator, opened and separated. The yolks should be beaten at a moderate pace while some of the corn meal batter is being beaten in—enough to make a fairly stiff paste. The egg whites should be beaten more rapidly, and, when they are a little stiffer than the yolks, *they* should be folded into the corn meal on top of the double boiler. The whole lot—milk, corn meal, egg yolks and whites—now should be mixed together and poured out into a good-sized pie plate. Fry the frankfurters gently in butter, place as many as you think you will need on top of the pie-to-be, and place them on top. Bake it at 350° until it is golden.

One weenie recipe that makes a good lunch or supper dish is a casserole made by taking four of the sausages cut in good-sized two-inch pieces, one-half cupful of chopped onions and the same amount of chopped pepper, and combining all these ingredients in a stew pan with about three tablespoonfuls of butter. Some flour should be added. Enough to thicken the whole thing. Two cups of milk, while your stirring-arm is getting even stiffer than it was in the last recipe. Pretty soon it will get thick. Turn off the stove for the moment.

Meanwhile, be getting out one container of creamed cottage

cheese and one cup of pre-cooked macaroni. Be stern about getting them to know each other by stirring them into the stew pan mixture. Take two more frankfurters and cut them first lengthwise in half, then crosswise at their centers. Arrange these pieces as though you were inventing the spoked wheel and bake the whole thing at about 350° for something under an hour.

The great thing, apart from its flavor, about the frankfurter is that it can be pressed into service very quickly and will perform like a member of Henry IV's private guard.

Cut up eight or ten slices of bacon with the kitchen shears. Take four lengthwise-sliced frankfurters and cook them with the bacon until the latter is crisp. Spoon off some fat and throw in one-half of a cupful of well-diced onion. Pour in a can of chicken broth, and approximately one teaspoonful of celery salt. Now, add a package of French's or Betty Crocker's dehydrated potatoes—the cubed kind, not the mashed. Stir in one can of whole kernel corn and add about one and one-half cups of milk. Stir together and let it heat to the boiling point, but do not allow it to boil. Serve it as close to the boiling point as you can.

There is a second quick soup that the ingenious wife, or even the ingenious bride, or even one of those ingenious bachelor girls whom Helen Gurley Brown is always advising to lead a swinging sex life, can put together with practically no trouble.

Take two cans of beef broth and one can of water, two minced cloves of garlic, two tablespoonfuls of butter, about a tablespoonful of dried basil, salt and pepper, three good-sized julienned carrots, and two small onions, each about the size of a balled-up handkerchief in the pocket of a first grader.

Simmer this, and while it is trying to find out what it is, cut up four frankfurters and about a pound of zucchini. Cut the frankfurters rather more thickly than the squash. Quarter four or five tomatoes. Do not bother to peel them. You may seed them, if you wish, but both seeding and peeling tomatoes are time-wasting endeavors. The skin of the tomatoes will fall off eventually, and you can pull it out of the pot with a fork or tweezers. After this soup has simmered for about twenty minutes, add the frankfurters and tomatoes and zucchini and stay away from it for another ten or fifteen minutes. Add one chicken bouillon cube, if you wish.

A lady I know has an even quicker method for the hallowed *wurst* in soup. She opens a can of Campbell's bean-and-bacon, adds a can of water, and slices in four or five frankfurters. Before serving, she shoots it through with dashes of Lea & Perrins. After she has done this, I hit my own portion with the Tabasco, a dash or two. Not everybody likes Tabasco as much as I do, and so I generally just pass the bottle when it is time to sit around the mildly complaining board.

Yet another fast dish, a rather more substantial one, can be made and done in roughly the time it takes to decide you are weary of Huntley and Brinkley—about three to ten minutes. Shred or grate a head of cabbage, put it in a skillet with butter or lard until it gets brownish, and add to it one-third of a cup of white vinegar and one-quarter of a cup of brown sugar, plus two teaspoonfuls of carroway seed and two of celery salt and one of plain old salt. Stir all this into the cabbage. Put eight frankfurters or more on top. Cover the dish and let it go for less than ten minutes. It may be garnished with celery leaves or parsley. I like to shower mine with soy sauce, using a heavy hand.

On nights when neither husband nor wife nor child feels like cooking, macaroni and frankfurters may be trotted out. The macaroni, elbow kind, is cooked first and put in a greased baking dish. One-half of a cup of milk is blended with one teaspoonful of Lea & Perrins, and this is poured over. Then add one can of Campbell's cheddar cheese soup. There should be two or three frankfurters which have been cut into very thin slices. Put the slices of frankfurters on top of the soup. This is known, God help us all, as Polka-Dotted Macaroni and Cheese. It came out of the Betty Crocker Kitchen, and sometimes I wish the name had not. But it really is quite good.

A little more expensive and a little slower to make, is a dish called Frankly Peppered Potato Bake. (They get pretty fly around the General Mills plants out there in Minneapolis, Minnesota.)

Cook one cup of chopped onion in three tablespoonfuls of butter. Add a teaspoonful of garlic powder or a smashed garlic clove, three cupfuls of peeled and diced potatoes, two teaspoonfuls of carroway seeds, the same amount of paprika, as much salt as you feel you need (about one teaspoonful ought to do), one can of tomato soup, and, finally, one pound of frankfurters, each cut into one-half inch slices. Put all this into a baking dish, cover it with aluminum foil, and bake at 350° for about one and one-quarter hours.

Mexican frankfurters are not much good unless they are imported from the U.S., but the Mexicans know how to do them if they can get their hands on some of the better products.

They combine about one-third of a cup of chili sauce, and either one tablespoonful of chili peppers, the dried kind, or a couple of dashes of Tabasco, and consign that to a stewpan on the stove. While that is heating, they cook the frankfurters in water that has been boiling-point-heated and turned off. They drain the frankfurters and put them in buns that have been toasted gently. Pour over them the sauce and shredded lettuce and cheese—Swiss, Cheddar or Gouda. Be more generous to your dachshunds with the cheese than with the lettuce. Some grated onion goes well, too, and perhaps some grated black olives. With this, I would serve forth some Mexe-Beans, El Paso brand.

Another bean and frankfurter dish with a southwestern flavor involves four or six or eight or ten or ten to fourteen frankfurters done the usual boiling-point way.

Combine a large can of lima beans and their liquid with a large can of kidney beans, also with their liquid. Parboil and chop one cupful of shredded cheese, either Cheddar, or of all things, Roquefort. If you use the latter, use only one-half cupful.

Cover the bottom of a casserole with some of the bean mixture. Gently muddle around with a wooden spoon. Put some frankfurters over the bottom layer of the mixed beans, add another layer of beans, more frankfurter pieces, and more beans again, and wind up with frankfurters on top. Bake, uncovered, for about thirty minutes at 250° by which time the beans will be bubbling and the frankfurters will be brown.

Some people like to top this with grated cheese. I don't. If you must use cheese, use the ever-popular Cheddar on top. Do not use Roquefort or Parmesan, please. Roquefort is fine *in* the casserole, but it is just too assertive on top.

Will these bean-frankfurter recipes never end? It seems to me that I have been writing them since puberty. Yet more are to come.

The Hebrew National people, who make all-beef frankfurters which are pretty good, if you like that kind, and whose wares are under the supervision of Rabbi Juda Altusky, have a pamphlet they will send if you write to 172-184 South Elliott Place, Brooklyn, New York 11217. Here are two of my favorites out of the pamphlet.

FRANKFURTER CORNSTICKS: All you do is pour a cornpone batter in a lengthwise cornpone pan, slit the frankfurters lengthwise, top the batter with them, and then cover with the rest of the batter. Relatives from the Deep South will like this one.

PRONTO DOGS: This recipe advises you to dip frankfurters into a mixture of one cupful of pancake mix and three-quarters of a cupful of water, and fry them in deep fat until they are brown. The dogs should be served hot, according to the pamphlet, which evidently was written for brides. I can't imagine serving them cold.

A nice variation on this consists of breaking four or five eggs into a bowl and whisking them well. Now, take a platter and put about a can of Progresso Bread Crumbs on it. These bread crumbs are made of toasted bread crumbs flavored with imported Italian cheese (Romano, if my palate is reliable), spices (the label doesn't say what kind), parsley, rare herbs (the label is mum about them, too, but I can detect oregano and thyme, which are hardly rare), and monosodium glutamate.

Dip the dogs into the eggs—to which you can add about four tablespoonfuls of milk, whisking again—then roll them in the crumbs, dip them into the egg mixture again, and roll them again in the crumbs. Place on waxed paper on another platter. Put about one cupful of Crisco or Wesson oil or any other reliable oil—with olive oil being the best—into a skillet and heat until the oil is hot. Let the dogs get brown all over, but not too brown. Goes well with tossed salad.

Back to ordinary pork-and-beef frankfurters. There are some really elaborate dishes that can be made with the utilitarian and versatile little *hund*, among them a kind of Americanized *paella*. This one takes real work. Well, a certain amount of it.

Chop one-half pound of fresh pork butt or lean bacon and add at least one pound of frankfurters which have been simmered for, oh, ten minutes, in water and then sliced about one inch. Put these in a large skillet, at least a 10-or-12 inch one, and pour two tablespoonfuls of oil, olive if you have it, over the ingredients. Sauté the pork and chopped frankfurters until they are nicely browned.

Fat will come out of the bacon, and some may ooze from the sausages. Pour this fat into a large flameproof casserole. Slice one large onion and two large green peppers, and set them aside. In the fat, brown eight chicken drumstcks, or four drumsticks, and four thighs. Brown very slowly, turning them often. When you think they have browned enough, throw in the onions and peppers, cover the casserole, and cook until the vegetables are tender. This takes about ten minutes.

Now add four-and-a-quarter cupfuls of either beef or chicken stock, made with cubes—the stock can be half chicken and half beef. Add the sliced frankfurters and chopped pork or bacon, and also pour in one-half cupful of very dry white wine. To this add two or three cloves of garlic, smashed to bits with the side of your cleaver on a chopping board, one teaspoonful of paprika, one-quarter teaspoonful of ground coriander, one bay leaf, one-half teaspoonful of thyme and the same amount of sage, and three-quarters of a teaspoonful of saffron.

To all this may be added one pound of boiled and shelled

shrimp, one tablespoonful of lemon juice, salt and pepper, two or three medium-sized tomatoes, quartered, two cups of green peas (use fresh ones, if possible, but canned will do), a can of drained pimentoes, a can of drained chick peas and, if you're really going all-out, about two dozen cherrystone clams. Do not open the clams.

Boil all this for about ten minutes, and then put in, spoonful by spoonful, two cupfuls of rice. Italian or Spanish rice are preferred by *paella* cooks, and the real nuts on the subject also add about two dozen mussels. Turn down the heat a little, so that the liquid is just simmering, and the rice is absorbing it. Do not stir too often. When the liquid is just about used up, the dish is ready. Carry it to the table in the casserole, and garnish the top of it with lemon wedges and parsley. You might sprinkle some paprika on it, as well.

This is a variation of a recipe devised by that empress of the kitchen *nonpareil*, Julia Child, and I have somewhat simplified it for you, although you will not notice the simplification, I am afraid, while you are putting it together. Takes time—you'd better allow yourself two hours.

For those whose appetite for the frankfurter is such that there are not enough recipes for preparing it in here, there is an excellent book called *The Hot Dog Cookbook*. It came out some years ago, but is still in print. It recommends, as I do, that frankfurters be obtained, if possible, from small establishments that make their own and do not ship them. That is not to say, as I most emphatically do not, that those put out and shipped all across the country and abroad by the big packing companies—Swift, Armour, Hormel, Cudahy, and the lot—are not good. They are very good indeed, hot or cold—plain coins of hot dogs on saltines, perhaps sprinkled with cheese—grated—or topped with an anchovy, make excellent *hors d'oeuvres*.

FRENCH TOAST AND SAUSAGE. A young man of my acquaintance, Rodney Chapman by name, came to my home after school at 3:30 and could not wait for dinner, which I like to eat anywhere between 8 and 10—sometimes, even 11, for I have Spanish blood. He decided to make himself some French toast and forthwith mixed the standard batter: two eggs, one-half teaspoonful of salt, one tablespoonful of sugar, and one-quarter cupful of milk, all of which he mixed in a shallow bowl with a whisk, meanwhile browning some butter in a skillet.

"Want some?" he asked. I said "No," then reconsidered.

He was browning his French toast in the butter, and when he turned the slices of bread over, they looked so good I changed my mind. I got another skillet, took two Jones Farm sausages, and split them lengthwise. While they were browning in my skillet, I took two slices of bread and dipped them in the boy's batter and fried them in *his* skillet. He already was eating his with the avidity of a black panther devouring a hartebeest.

When my French toast was done, I took it out and set it on a plate, both slices, side by side. The sausages were done. I took them and laid them on one of the slices, went to the refrigerator and found some cranberry sauce, and put that sparingly over the sausages. Other preserves could be used. So could a banana, sliced lengthwise.

Now, I covered the first slice with the second and put tooth-picks in the sandwich to secure it.

Dipping it all in the batter again, I then went on to frying it gently on both sides, just as the boy had done. This gave me a double-thick coating of the delightful French toast mixture, and it was, in sum, nothing short of delicious.

This sandwich could be made with loose sausage as well as links. It also could be enhanced, and made into a mountainous edifice, by the addition of a layer of grated cheese—Cheddar, preferably sharp, or Edam, or Swiss. Sometimes I consider getting some Stilton and adding it, for I am certain that the flavors of the sausage and that noble English cheese would go very well together.

Raw tomatoes, sliced very thin, and onions, also sliced thin, could go nicely on the plate, but if the tomatoes are added, with or without the onions, another slice of French toast should be added to make the sandwich a three-decker.

When I began experimenting with this sandwich I thought of numerous other things to add to it. Sometimes I behave the way Dagwood used to behave in the old comic strip. I get carried away by the contents of the refrigerator, and my quest for culinary experimentation rivals that of Bell, Edison, and other innovators, although from what I have read of their lives, I gather that none of those pioneers ever ate much. Anchovies would taste good if put beneath the tomato-onion third slice of toast. So would a good hearty slice of Lebanon bologna. So, for that matter, would a couple of slices of prosciutto, that marvelous Italian pepper-encrusted ham, or Smithfield ham, or Kentucky ham.

The whole thing, however, boils down to the sausage taste, or fries down to it, as you wish. Pimentoes may be laid over the sausages, if you are making the simple two-decker. So may black olives. And now that we're talking of olives, the whole thing can take on a faintly Moorish-Spanish-Italian flavor if cooked in olive oil rather than butter. If you do do it in this oil, make sure the oil does not get too hot before you put in the French toast sandwich.

GEFÜLTE BRÖTCHEN. The Viennese eat a great deal of sausage, but it is not always encased in intestines. Sometimes, as the size of so many men walking the streets amply demonstrates, the sausage is encased in rich, fattening bread.

This item, which is one of those *brötchen* specialties of Alt Wien, makes a fine lunch, one that is so easy to prepare it makes its maker want to stand up and do a waltz, possibly *The Skaters'*.

Take a long roll of crusty bread and cut off both noses. Save them to dice later and use either as croutons or stuffing. Hollow out the bread either with a long slicing knife or a narrow spoon. Put anchovy paste in the cave you have made, having mixed the paste first with generous teaspoonfuls of butter. I cannot give exact proportions here because I do not know what size roll you are going to use.

The buttered rolls, or loaf, should be set in the refrigerator and allowed to remain there for about an hour. While it is in there, shivering and wishing it were back in the bakery, you can be getting on with the rest of the proceedings.

In the grinder, force out about a pound of cooked or smoked ham, fat included, the same amount of roast veal, and the same amount of smoked tongue. Now grind these members of the wedding together, or mix them in a bowl with a heavy wooden spoon.

Meanwhile, be frying three or four slices of bacon which have come from some reliable purveyor. Fry them until they are crisp and can be crumbled. Reduce three hard-cooked eggs to a pulp, mercilessly, and do the same thing to a large dill pickle, one which a sensitive, God-fearing nose could detect a mile away, so strong will the garlic be. Open a can of Portuguese sardines and pulp them with your mortar and pestle. Chop about one-quarter of a cupful of pistacchio nuts. Now mix all the ingredients and put them through the grinder again, and then stuff the bread tubes, or the rolls, with what comes out. Pack the stuffing in tightly, and if you have any left over, hollow out another piece of bread.

Wrap these bread-encased sausages in wax paper, Saran Wrap, or foil, and put them back in the refrigerator for about one hour before you are planning to eat them.

Sometimes, when making this, I have added mustard, usually dry. Not too much—only a pinch or two. As much salt and pepper as I think the mixture needs.

Practically speaking, short rolls, about four inches long, are better than a long loaf of bread, for the rolls are easier to hollow out. A long loaf may be sliced, however, and because it is wider than a roll, will give you more room for the stuffing. The proportions of the ingredients may be increased as you judge you will need them: two hardboiled eggs, two dill pickles, more meat, etc.

A good side dish to Gefülte Brötchen can be made as follows. After you have hollowed out the bread and put it in the refrigerator the first time, and while the bacon is getting itself crisp, open a large can of kidney beans. Put the beans in a colander and let cold water sparkle over them. Wait until the water has drained out of the colander and then let the beans dry a bit. Into an earthen casserole put one-half cupful of olive oil and one of wine vinegar, a crushed bayleaf, two cloves of garlic forced through a press, salt and pepper, some thyme and some parsley sprigs. Muddle the ingredients well with a wooden spoon, then add the beans and gently work the marinade in and around them. Add some more sprigs of parsley, and forget it for about a half hour. Then put it into the refrigerator until you are ready to serve the Brötchen.

When the Brötchen is nicely chilled, take it out and put it on a plate. Arrange a spoonful of kidney beans on a leaf of lettuce on the side. You need nothing more for a festive lunch, except something to drink.

GREEN BEANS AND SAUSAGE.   It is hard to keep Mrs. Oscar Luecke, of Columbia, Pennsylvania, out of this book. She is in it the way marbling is in a good piece of beef. She is in it so much, other housewives in the Pennsylvania Dutch area are going to go up and paint hex signs on her house.

One of the best recipes she sent me was this one, which asks you to combine about one and one-half pounds of loose sausage, one chopped onion about the size of an old-fashioned glass paperweight, a chopped pepper about the same size, and one-half cup of chopped celery which you have previously stripped with that kitchen tool, the name of which I always forget. Form all this into inch-and-a-quarter balls and brown them in a casserole.

Pour off a little of the fat which the sausages will sweat out. Add one-and-one-half cups of fresh tomatoes, cut into quarters, or one large can, liquid and all. Add two pounds of destringed green beans. Also, eight small, preferably new, potatoes.

Cover the pot and put on the stove top. It will require at least forty-five minutes to get itself done, but while that is happening you can take a short nap, meanwhile wondering if you should have added one-half cup of water. I daresay you should have, especially if you have not used *canned* tomatoes. The fresh ones carry a good deal of water, but not that much.

In this dish, broccoli could be substituted for the green beans. Or cauliflower. I would serve it with some crusty mop-up bread, the thicker the better. Afterward, I would put out some sort of fruit compote, touched with champagne or a sparkling white wine, and then I would pass around cigars to the men and hie the ladies off to their own corner of the room to talk about their plans for governing the world.

HACIENDA DINNER. One day in Mexico, I happened into a tiny town, where I asked a man the name of the place to get the best chili. "El Paso, Texas," he said. That night I fell in with a group of laborers hanging around a bar. Having not had time to go to El Paso, let alone to Cuernavaca, which was my destination, I asked one of them to direct me to a place where I could get some good Mexican food.

"Come home with me," he said. "My wife will make you something to eat."

We had what my new friend called a hacienda dinner. It was something that anybody in the United States, or any other country for that matter, could duplicate without undue exertion. The recipe goes roughly as follows:

Brown about a pound of loose sausage and then drain off some of the grease. Add one cupful each of chopped onion and chopped green pepper. Add to that one large can of tomatoes, preferably Italian ones, and one-half cupful of some kind of barbecue sauce or A-1 Sauce.

Now take one package of Kraft, if you will excuse the expression, Dinner, available in most supermarkets and grocery stores. Empty this into the sausage-and-onion mixture, which by this time should be as angry as a Van Nuys, California, citizen who has just been bilked again by one of the local used car dealers. Do not cook the Kraft Dinner first. Dump it right in. Cover it and simmer it for about twenty minutes. This recipe does not call for stock but, if I were you, I would put in a bouillon cube or two and perhaps a cupful of milk, rather than water. The milk, you might find upon experimentation, may make this a little thicker than you wish. If so, next time stick

84

to water and add about one-half to three-quarters of a teaspoon of cornstarch.

This dish requires nothing on the side except, possibly, a shaker of chili powder, some salt and pepper, and a bowlful of raw onions and tomatoes, and a large slice of orange for each plate. If you can find some hot green or red peppers, they go well with it, especially if you have marinated them in some old vinegar for three or four days.

Link sausage will do well enough for this dish, but not as well as the loose. Ordinary elbow macaroni will do as well as Kraft Dinner, and you can use any packaged or freshly-grated parmesan cheese along with it.

You can do this up in true Mexican style by taking a can of drained kidney beans, or pinto beans, lacing them liberally with some red wine, putting them into a skillet, and crushing them with the heel or back of a spatula. The beans then ought to be refried until they are as pulpy as Carmine Basilio's face used to be after one of his more arduous matches. On the other hand, a firm called Old El Paso makes canned refried beans, which—if you can find them—will save you all the trouble. The refried beans are served as a side dish. They are enhanced by grated cheese, as well. This lunch, or breakfast, or whatever, certainly is going to give your cheese grater a workout, which ought to make it grateful. (Oooh.)

HAGGIS. This is the well-known Scottish dish, eaten, God knows why, by Scotsmen everywhere. "It is a sort of Paleolithic Sausage," said Gerald Kersh, who may have taken on some of his caveman tendencies by gulping it down in childhood. You are going to need a strong stomach to eat this stomach. Kersh was explicit about its preparation. No, not explicit. Stubborn, obdurate, unrelenting.

"You take the large and the small stomach bag of a lamb, wash the large one in water and then fight it into boiling water. Leave it out overnight to soak in cold water. Take it out in the morning and turn the inside out. Wash the small bag, and the liver, heart and lights of the lamb, and boil for one and a half hours in water to cover it. Leave the windpipe hanging out of the pot to let out any impurities that may be present. When you take the stuff out of the pot, cut away the gristle and the pipe. Mince the heart and lights, and grate half the liver. Mix this with about one-half pound of chopped suet, three finely-chopped onions, oatmeal and pepper. Add as much of the cooking liquid as will make it into a good pliable mixture, and stuff it into the large bag. Sew it up tightly and boil it for three hours in a large pot, covered, of course, with water."

There will be leftover lights, heart and grated liver. Place what is left over, plus some more chopped onion and more of the seasonings into the smaller stomach. Boil that, too. Both bags will begin to swell under the boiling, and they should be pricked lightly. By the time you get the second bag in, you should try to be at your neighbor's house, at least a half mile away, having a drink. This must be done out of self-preservation.

What to serve on the side of a haggis sausage? Hell, I don't know. Horseradish, perhaps. Some people put bread crumbs in it—very stale ones. If you do not do that, you might try some new potatoes, boiled in their jackets. Both stomachs may be warmed up if they are steamed or steeped for approximately one-half hour.

HEAD SAUSAGE. One time, Wild Bill Davison, the jazz cornetist, and I were in a restaurant in Plymouth, England. As he sat down, he said to the waitress who came to serve us, "May I see the head waitress?"

The head waitress appeared, a most imposing lady, standing at least as high as the doorway.

"Are you the head waitress?" Davison inquired.

"Yes, sir," she said.

"Fine," said the irrepressible Davison. "I'll have some head."

The vulgarity of this palaver escaped her, but she brought us some head cheese, garnished with smashed hard-boiled eggs, pickles, and a *vinaigrette* sauce to pour over it. That was not quite what Davison had in mind, but he choked it down manfully.

At home, a few months later, I essayed a head sausage.

Going to a butcher shop near Manganaro's, that wonderful grocery on Ninth Avenue in New York, I bought a calf's head and a pig's head, having the butcher remove the eyes, but making certain that he removed the brains and saved them for me. I also bought a calf's tongue.

I took the two heads and the tongue home and, with a couple of kitchen matches, singed the hair off the ears of both heads, trying not to look at them in that process. The heads were plunged into boiling water which contained a carrot stripped of its outer skin, an onion stuck with two whole cloves, a bay leaf, a few sprigs of parsley, and some sage and thyme in very small pinches. Then went in about one-half tablespoonful of coarsely ground salt, plus two or three twists of pepper out of the mill.

Heads must be boiled for a long time. About three hours may be enough time, depending upon their size, but it is better to do them for four, at least. At the midway point, put in the tongue, which only takes half as long. Drain the whole thing. Save the liquid, which will be a good basic soup stock with a couple of bouillon cubes thrown in.

Put the heads and the tongue on the carving board and, with your sharpest knife, cut them into long slices of meat. Use the ears, as well as everything else that may come up from the skulls. The cheek meat is especially good. While the meat is lying there quivering on the chopping board or block, get out your meat grinder. You will have bought some bung, or casing, either beef or pork, from a butcher who knows about such matters. Put the meat in a bowl.

Season the calf's and pig's heads well—with cracked peppercorn, with some fennel seed, and with—oh, the Lord preserve us!—a dash of sherry. Break in a fresh egg. Muddle together the contents of the bowl as well as you can.

The casing, or bung, meanwhile, will have been soaking in cold, salted water while the heads have been cooking. Take the casings out and affix them to the no-nonsense end of your grinder which, I hope, is a sensible one that has to be turned by hand. Put a fine blade into the grinder and begin feeding in the slivers of calf's head, pig's head, and tongue from which you will have removed the membrane.

The various members of this sausage family should be fed to the grinder in this order: calf, pig, tongue, calf, pig, tongue. Discard that bay leaf. It is too assertive, and should be disposed of after it has done its initial duty in the boiling pot.

Grind in some more cracked pepper as you are going through this enervating process. Not too much. About four or five peppercorns at the most. You might grind in a chopped red pepper as well—not the very hot kind, but one which will add color to your sausage. Also, you could grind in a clove of garlic which you have chopped beforehand and added to the sausage at the rate of every four or five links.

After you have put the slices of the heads and the tongue through the grinder one time, put them through again. This will mix them, and the pepper, and the garlic, and everything else, in an indescribable manner. Now put them through again. Yes, for the third time, and then grind them back into the bung. By this time, your grinding-arm will be so tired you will be cursing not just me but all the Lancaster butchers who taught me how to make this time-consuming sausage. They, in turn, are cursing their grandfathers, who taught them how to make it.

Now, tie up the sausage in about ten-inch lengths, and hang it in your smokehouse, if you have one, or in the portable smokehouse, mentioned before, that may be obtained from any good hardware store. If you haven't got either, you can build a fire in your fireplace, let it get down to embers, and hang the lengths of the encased meat on hooks which you previously have attached to the walls of the chimney. Throw water on the coals. This will send up the smoke you need for curing. Take the sausages down after about three hours and hang them in a cold, dry place for about two weeks. After that, put them in the fireplace and repeat the process all over.

During all this time, you will be able to weed your garden,

try to read *War and Peace*, play either sixteen sets of tennis or eighteen games of nine-ball, smoke thirty-six packages of cigarettes, and take at least three shots (the tender kind, not the gun kind) at your neighbor's wife or his ox.

The sausage must then be put back in the same cool, dry place. Again it must be hauled out and smoked. By now it will be black from all that smoke. Links should be cut away from their restraining string and placed in the friendly refrigerator. This sausage can be eaten cold or it can be pan-fried. I would recommend it cold, sliced down, and served forth with fairly thick onion rings and horseradish. Good in sandwiches, if you can find some honest-to-God Lancaster County Swiss cheese made by the Amish. You will not find this head sausage on the Amish markets, by the way, or in any other market anywhere in the world. I invented it, and if you want to try it, you will have to do it this way or invent it yourself. The butchers showed me the way, but it is *mine!*

Head cheese, that old reliable, is made much in the same way, except that after slicing the meat of the heads and tongue, you do not put it through the grinder. You chop it into coarse pieces, and perhaps add some leftover ham, or some roast beef, or pot roast cubes. While you are dicing the slices of calf's head, pig's head, and tongue, you should be simmering the stock they cooked in with the addition of one chicken and one beef bouillon cube.

Now pitch the bits of meat, with perhaps some leftover chicken, into a pan that would nicely suit a loaf of bread. Add to the stock one tablespoonful of Knox Gelatin (is there any other kind?) and pour it over the meat cubes until the stock rises about one-quarter inch above the latter. Salt and pepper this liberally. Cover it with a cheesecloth and set aside to cool for a while.

When it is so cool that Dizzy Gillespie's music would sound fairly hot beside it, put it into the refrigerator, placing an old-fashioned iron, or some other weight, perhaps a barrette once worn by Lois DeFee, the lady bouncer, over the cheesecloth-covered head cheese.

You must now have something else for supper, for the head cheese, which is a kind of sausage, must be allowed to remain in the refrigerator for at least 24 hours. This will jell it as it needs to be jelled, and you can slice it down and serve it to your wife, or your guests, or whoever is present (if you *are* a wife, it may be your husband). They probably will not like it much. Women like aspics, for some reason I never have been able to unravel, but they seldom like jelled meats.

Smash up some hard-cooked eggs, and mince some pickles, and float them in two jiggers of oil and one of vinegar, and pour that sauce over the head cheese, once it is jelled and cool. This may not make the diners shout with delight at first. To tell the truth, head cheese is not very appetite-apprehending on initial view. But once they try it, they will be more than satisfied. Exclamations of appreciation will be heard.

ITALIAN SAUSAGES IN RED WINE. First you go and buy your red wine. It must be a cheap Chianti. The liquor dealer will ask you what kind. Tell him not to be foolish. He then will offer a California brand. Tell him that is very nice but you are looking for something a little more foreign. Strum some stringed instrument, if you know how to play one. Twist your moustache, if you happen to have one. If you do not, grow one for the occasion. He will offer you Bolla Bardolino, which is first-rate, but which is not—definitely not—what you are looking for. Then he will offer you Valpolicella, which is even more expensive.

"Haven't you got one that sells for something like $1.56 per half-gallon?" you will ask.

"No," he will say.

You will now settle for the California brand. You will not like it, but you will not mind too much, for you are using it only for cooking.

Now go out and get some Italian link sausage. Which brings us again to the dilemma of To Prick Or Not To Prick. In the case of Italian sausage, prick. They are so laden with fat and fatty juices, you will be better off allowing them to fry in their own contents. If you wait until they are half-done to prick them, you will very likely get some fat right in the eye.

Presuming you can find some Italian sausages, which is not much of a chore in any city with an Italian neighborhood, place them in a frying pan, prick and coil the others around one sausage placed in the center. Or place them in a shallow casserole. These sausages are so rich, it is advisable to prick pronto and allow them all to cook or fry in the fat.

Pour about one-half cupful of wine over them. These fat

gentlemen, looking like Milanese businessmen, should be permitted to get themselves drunk in that wine, so drunk that they will get as brown as an Italian colonial soldier. This will take about twenty minutes or one-half hour on medium-high heat.

The best thing to send out to diners with this dish is buttered noodles or macaroni. And, if you can get them, pieces of finnochio on the side, bathed in equal parts of oil and vinegar, dusted with tiny pinches of oregano and generous sprinklings of parsley, fresh or dried.

A friend of mine sometimes grates provolone cheese over the sausage before he serves it, and if he has no provolone, he grates old hard Gouda or Swiss. This seems to me to be a little much, since there will already be some grated cheese on the noodles. It is better, I think, to keep the cheese off the sausage, but it all depends on what your family thinks.

Some people often present their guests with a tomato sauce, or stewed tomatoes, either atop or aside of the sausage. Others hand out green peppers, fried in chunks. This, I think, is silly. Crusty bread from a good Italian or French bakery, yes. Various sauces, no.

This dish may also be made with American pork links, although not with the success that the Italian varieties command. It can be made with rice instead of pasta or even served with mashed or French-fried potatoes.

The great, great thing about sausage is that it has an adaptability that virtually no other meat can equal. It can be used with nearly any kind of vegetable or fruit, and if it is made well, it will be acceptable to all. Unless it is presented in scrapple. No, I have not mentioned it thus far, but I hate scrapple. I will mention it later.

ITALIAN SAUSAGES WITH PASTA. What more reasonable a recipe, I asked myself one night, could the hand of man devise? Italian sausages, hot or sweet? Pasta? Elbow macaroni, long and even limp spaghetti, the broadbreasted hunks of pasta that are put into lasagna, my God, even vermicelli—how could a man go wrong?

This recipe *sounds* fairly simple, but beware of it. Perhaps you would be better off if you opened a can of something by Franco-Amercan and tried that. Then you could curse the canned food instead of me. However, he said, with jaunty insouciance, do not despair.

Get some Italian sausages, about two for each guest. One sweet, one hot, for each person. There are two theories for cooking these gentlemen. Some people say they ought to be done on the griddle, sautéed lightly, at once. Other people maintain that they ought to be cooked in water at first, and then pricked or poked after the water has boiled off. I lean to the latter notion. In any case, they ought to be browning.

While the sausages are traipsing off to the done state, you can be boiling some water—oh, about a gallon of it—into which you have previously put about one teaspoonful of salt and two chicken bouillon cubes. If you happen to have some leftover chicken around, that is even better, provided it has not been fried. Chicken that has been fried is not much good for stock.

When the water is boiling as angrily as Charles de Gaulle, add two cups of whatever pasta you are planning to use. The pasta will require about seven, eight, or nine minutes to get itself to the *al dente* state. Elbow macaroni may take a little longer. So may the pasta which manufacturers persist in calling Wagon Wheels. Kids like them because they enjoy playing with them. But they are not suitable fare for adults.

Now while the macaroni, or whatever pasta you are having, is being boiled in its pot, shove the sausage aside in its frying pan, and thin-slice some green or red pepper, some tomato, some onion, and sprinkle all this with small pinches of parsley, oregano, marjoram and salt. Do not permit the vegetables to get brown in the grease. When the onions are golden, and the aroma is rising, yank everything off the burners.

Take the pasta and put it in a colander and run cold water over it. No, not on the stove, in the sink. When the pasta has been drained, lay it over the simmering sausages, over the vegetables, and with a good big chef's knife cut the sausages into sections of about one inch. Muddle all this stuff together, and pray. If you are daring, at this point, you now may add about one ounce of red or white wine. Or a shot of brandy or bourbon. Sprinkle on more parsley—but no more oregano, please—and some Romano or Parmesan cheese.

Broiled eggplant goes well with this dish. Just brush eggplant halves with oil, salt and pepper them with a retiring hand, and set them under the broiler while the sausages are cooking and the pasta is getting ready to be eaten. Or you can use Zucchini the same way, splitting it. Summer squash will also do. Winter squash, never. Winter squash is not good under any circumstances.

This Italian sausage dish can also be made, of course, with loose sausage, but it will not be as good. The bung, or natural casing, in which the Italian links come imparts a flavor that the loose sausage never achieves.

Peaches, grapes, peeled oranges and limes can be served as afterthoughts to this dish, well-bathed in Strega or Fiore de Alpe. Then small cups of strong coffee that look and smell as though they could have taken on Carmine Basilio in his prime.

J ESTENA EBERŞOLE'S SAUSAGE AND APRICOT DINNER. Mrs. Ebersole not only was nice enough to have a wild first name, she also gave me a wild sausage recipe. Watch out.

Sauté one-third of a cup of chopped onions. Once the onions have turned golden, add one-and-one-third cups of pre-cooked rice. Into that should go one twelve-ounce can of apricot nectar and one-half teaspoonful of salt. Mrs. Ebersole says you can use water if you can't find apricot nectar. But try. Bring the nectar-rice-onion mixture to a boil, stirring constantly. Then cook it over a very low heat.

Now, with a blaring of centurions' horns, come the magnificent sausages. *Smoked.* If they are not smoked, smoke them. Then cut them in half. I hope, for your sake, they are not frozen sausages. If they are, your knife-hand may slip and you will cut off one of your fingers. Beware of that. It will not taste good in this recipe, and you may find that you miss it.

Grill or bake the sausage halves. While they are going to work on themselves, you go to work heating some fresh or canned green beans cut on the bias, the way Chinese cooks cut them. Also cook one cupful of dried apricots, peeled and whole.

"Spoon rice into center of heated platter," says Mrs. Ebersole. "Surround it with the sausage halves, cooked apricots, and *drained* green beans. Garnish all this with parsley or watercress."

No side-dish vegetable really is needed with all this. The apricots supply the fruity taste. The rice takes the place of any potatoes you might think of serving. I face Pennsylvania and bow to Mrs. Jestena Ebersole.

K

EAGY SAUSAGE ROLLS. The trick to all successful sausage cookery is to keep it simple, and Mrs. Elwood Keagy, who lives in my home town of Lancaster, has got simplicity down to a science.

She takes twelve link sausages, each about the size of a troll's nose, and twelve slices of thin bread. While the sausages are happily going to their fiery doom under the broiler, she cuts the crusts off the bread. The sausages take about ten or twelve minutes to get the pleasant shade of brown they ought to be.

Now Mrs. Keagy rolls each one in one of the bread slices, securing them, I suppose, with a toothpick. Or perhaps the grease holds the bread. She then puts them back under the broiler until the bread is toasted. I would serve Major Grey's chutney with these warriors.

KURTZ PORK CHEESE CAKES. Mrs. Marvin Kurtz, a good cook I know who lives in Ephrata, Pennsylvania, where so many good cooks live, has a recipe for cakes or patties that a bride of two hours could do with her left hand. (Her right hand, presumably, would be caressing her husband.) Mrs. Kurtz takes one-and-one-half pounds of loose sausage and mixes it with one cupful of fine dry bread crumbs, and two-thirds of a cupful of "shredded" (I suppose she means grated) cheddar cheese. Use a good stout cheese from some country shop. Grate hell out of it.

Throw in two lightly beaten eggs. Mix all this together, with your hands. Shape the mixture into hamburger-like patties. Wrap each patty with a slice of bacon. Secure the bacon with a toothpick. Put on the oven rack above a shallow roasting pan. Bake for thirty or thirty-five minutes at 375°. Manna from Mrs. Kurtz.

96

LANGUEDOCIENNE SAUSAGES. It is impossible for me to tell where you are going to find Toulouse sausages in the United States, but if you are enterprising, and happen to know a French butcher in some big city, you may succeed. Sausages *à la languedocienne* are worth the effort.

Toulouse sausages are big ones in which the meat (pork and young calf) has been chopped by a butcher with an arm the size of a ham and then mixed with mace, nutmeg, salt, pepper, and a pinch of saltpeter. They have an invincible aroma and flavor. The next day you will know all too well that you ate them on the preceding day. Persevere and prevail. I am not going to tell you how to make Toulouse saucisses, because I really do not know how.

But if you can get some, twist them into a coil that will fit neatly into an iron pan in which you previously have put about three tablespoonfuls of goose grease. Now peel and then flatten, as usual with the side of your cleaver, four good-sized cloves of garlic. Throw in a *bouquet garni*. Put a lid on the pan and cook the sausage for approximately twenty minutes. Take out the coil of sausage and put it in a very low oven to keep warm.

Fast work is now required. Into the frying pan, put two tablespoonfuls of vinegar. While the sausages have been cooking, you will have been making a brown sauce roux of flour and some bouillon or a bouillon cube dissolved in water. Put this in with the vinegar and sausage grease, stirring as though you were a fireman on a World War I tanker. When all this is behaving as though it were Christmas, add one-half cupful of tomato puree. Let it all boil together for about five minutes, still stirring it. Four tablespoonfuls of pickled capers now join the frenzy. Add three or four tablespoonfuls of either dry or fresh parsley. Stir again and again and again and again. Remove the sausages from the warming oven. Pour your gravy all over

97

them. Serve. I like plain boiled rice with this. Or, sometimes, black-eyed peas. Good hard bread ought to be served so that the gravy can be sopped up.

It is not absolutely necessary for you to locate Toulouse sausages for this. Any coarsely-made sausages, even the Italian sweet or hot ones, will do. But, somehow, Toulouse sausages have a flavor that is distinctly their own.

LENTILS AND SAUSAGE. Nobody has any right to tell the modern *hausfrau*, young or old, how to cook lentils, least of all your Beloved American Journalist here, who now reminds his readers that this flat, brown member of the pease, or peas, family is often overlooked as the root for substantial, inexpensive meals, which can also be delicious. A lady can make enough lentils and sausage to feed six for less than $2 without spending much time in the kitchen.

Get one cup of dried lentils, wash them and pick them over, and put them in water to cover at about the time the late evening news is over. Let them lie there drowning all night long.

At about ten o'clock the next morning, the lentils should be drained, but the liquid in which they have been soaking should be saved. Two cupfuls of this should now be heated without too much vehemence. While it is moiling itself around above the flame, the cook should be mincing or chopping an onion about half the size of the ball used in a game of *jai alai*, and simultaneously cutting up two or three sprigs of parsley. I am assuming that all my readers are ambidexterous. One clove of garlic should also be rent asunder, and so should one stalk of celery, including the leaves. Some salt should be waiting in the wings—about two teaspoonfuls of it—and a pepper grinder should be there chafing to get in.

All these ingredients are added to the lentil liquid, and so should the lentils themselves, and all of these gentle and uncomplaining friends should be allowed to simmer, covered— *not* to boil—for about fifteen or twenty minutes. Lentils must not be boiled into submission.

While all the simmering is taking place, there should be two other operations going on.

98

Some sausages—as many as you think you will need—should be snarling vociferously in a frying pan or on a home-made Reynolds Wrap pan under the broiler. It seems to me that the frying-pan method is better, if only because you can start the links in a half-inch of water. Let that steam away and—well, no sausage cook needs be given this advice—the sausages ought to come out brown.

The second operation involves greasing or oiling a good-sized baking dish, or casserole, or Corning Ware receptacle. I like to use an earthen pot I once picked up in France. I use this for nothing but lentils and beans. Like old French chefs and their omelette-spiders, I never wash it, except on the outside. I wipe out the inside with an old but clean shirt.

In a colander, over another pan, drain the cooked lentil mixture. Once again, save the liquid.

Now that I am writing it down, I find that this dish is so much trouble to make, Jim Beard himself might shun it.

Once the lentils, onions, parsley, *et al.*, are removed, some fat, preferably sausage grease or olive oil, should be put into a saucepan. About one tablespoonful of flour should be stirred in with a whisk, and to that should be added a little better than one cupful of the lentil juice. All this should be whisked as though you were uncontrolable.

Meanwhile, you have placed the lentils in that baking dish you greased or oiled beforehand. When the gravy is nicely thickened, pour it over the lentils.

Now rescue the sausages. Lay them, with the most infinite tenderness, atop the lentils. Slice two tomatoes, skinned or un-, each about the size of a Ringling Brothers' clown's nose. Salt them. Place them atop the sausages, as though they were straining to get down at the sausages, which, of course, they ultimately will do.

The lentils and sausages should be cooked, uncovered, at about 250° for at least two hours. From time to time, dashes of sherry—and I do mean dashes—should be added. Or of red wine. The idea is to keep the flavor of the sausages and the lentils, and to permit them to enjoy each other so that you will enjoy them.

Cook this dish for three hours, if you wish. The pigs that gave you the sausages are already dead, and so are the vines on which the lentils grew. They died for you. Why not give them the tribute of your enjoyment of them?

There is practically nothing that goes along with this dish, except some crusty French or Italian bread with which to mop up. Lentils and sausage need no accompaniment. The dish does need a good deal of work, and for that reason ought to be done on a Saturday or Sunday when you have time to concentrate on it.

LIEDERKRANZ UND SAUSAGE. One night, when I was working my way through a chapter of a novel that probably never should have been finished, I found myself hungry. This was a fairly unusual experience for me. When I am trying to work on fiction, I seldom eat. The conditions of the task are seldom conducive to eating, for eating requires cooking, and cooking requires time off from the typewriter.

I looked in the refrigerator. Tobin's, that estimable house of the encased meat product, had sent me some sausage, the plain pork kind, unfrilled and each link in its right little mind. I thought I would have some of them, with perhaps some scrambled eggs on the side, and some alternate rounds of green tomatoes and onion arranged near them, sprinkled over gently with some parsley, rosemary, oil and vinegar, and possibly a little oregano, not to mention salt, pepper, and monosodium glutamate.

I prepared the sausage links on the way back to my typewriter by starting them in a skillet with a small amount of water.

Three paragraphs later, I went back to have a look at them. The water had steamed itself off into the universe, and the sausage links were now browning nicely. I tried to turn them with a spatula, but they would not budge. I pricked them, and got little spurts of hot fat on my forearms and wrists for my trouble. The sausages did permit some of their grease to remain in the pan and now, as I turned down the heat, they permitted

100

me to roll them over. I turned it down still lower, and soon they were singing a seething song of ecstasy, as though awaiting my appetite. Nothing sounds better than a happy sausage.

Four more paragraphs. I was writing hastily, for I was so hungry I could have eaten one of the Jolly Green Giant's legs. Yet I did not feel hungry for eggs, scrambled, coddled, or fried.

I had some Jim Dandy grits around, but grits are a pain in the neck to make unless you have made them the day before. There was some leftover succotash in the refrigerator. No.

Cajoling the sausage links by turning them again, I went back to my monster and did three more paragraphs, all about the size of this one. They did not quite satisfy me, but they kept the typewriter quiet.

Back to the kitchen I went. The sausage fumes were now all but overpowering. Bluejays were beginning to cluster around the kitchen door, and the dachshund was off barking up his neighbors, inviting them in.

What am I going to eat with these links? I asked Myself— taking on the identity of The Deity. I did not know. I did not want eggs, that was clear. I could feel it in my stomach. This was not An Egg Morning. Stewed tomatoes? I thought not. Raw, yes, with onions, but not stewed, not even the Italian kind. Mushrooms? No, I'm afraid not.

Then the inspiration occurred to me. On the top of the refrigerator was a mighty plastic box containing all sorts of cheeses that I had forgotten to eat over a long period of time. I hauled down the box, which smelled so strong that it could have been used as a weapon against the crew of a flying saucer that recently had debarked from Arcturus. Inside it was some old, hard Cheddar, some Roquefort, a slab of Swiss that, if sliced properly, could have been used to shingle roofs, and some Liederkranz.

Many people believe that Liederkranz is an American cheese, which it is, but most people believe that it is a German cheese, for when it is right it can be smelled from Berlin to Milwaukee. It cannot be said that this cheese, when in full ripeness, can be smelled from San Francisco to Tokyo. Dogs have been known to turn their tails and whimper to be let outside when a small block of Liederkranz has been on the top of the refrigerator for three or four days. It is not a German or Swiss cheese, it is American, and was developed by the Borden Company long before their Daisy the cow became a symbol.

I got out my bag of clothespins, clamped one on my nose, and cut off some Liederkranz. This—the cheese, not the clothespin—I spread over my simmering sausage. I salted and peppered it, and, trembling in the full force of creation, sprinkled over some chopped shallots. Chopped scallions would have been all right, and so would chopped onions. Over all this, I sprinkled some bright red cayenne.

The Liederkranz melted, the sausages took it to their manly little bosoms, and with a couple of toasted slices of corn bread, I had a fine breakfast, although as I was eating it I reflected that I should have split the sausage before laying on the cheese. I did this the next time. Much better.

LIMA BEANS AND SAUSAGE.   One night I wandered into my cell-like kitchen, which was then lighted by a bulb that would seem to be better-suited for a prison cell. In the gloom I looked up at my shelves. There was a can of lima beans there. The refrigerator held, as it always does, some sausage, about four days home from the store. I hauled it out and browned it lightly. Opening the beans, I poured some of the sausage grease over them (only about a tablespoonful) in a stewpot, added a peeled and shredded onion to the remaining grease in the sausage pan and browned that fellow easily. I then added that to the beans and shook in some dried parsley. Fresh parsley would have been better; it always is. (Anything fresh is better than anything dried, dehydrated, or frozen.)

The sausages next were laid over the limas, who did not protest. I added two jiggers of cheap dry white wine. Then I touched this thing with as much dry mustard which, if it had been talcum powder, could have served at a newborn's diaper-changing. I let it simmer awhile. Then I grabbed the pot off the stove, ladled some of the creation into it, and got myself a spoon and a napkin, and, as an afterthought, a crust of French

102

bread that could not have been more than two days old. It needed salt and pepper. It needed something else, too, I later decided, and the next time I made this dish, I put in a quarter of a bay leaf, well pulverized. I also added two quartered tomatoes—or was it a small can of Italian tomatoes? I cannot remember. Anyhow, add tomatoes. Another time, I added some slivered green peppers. And, slave to the sauce that I am, I dashed in Tabasco with three hard moves of the wrist.

This could be done with red wine, but that would not bring out the true lima bean flavor. It also could be done with black-eyed peas.

LYON SAUSAGE. The first time I was in Lyon, I was nicely mugged and all the francs were stolen out of my wallet. This did not matter much, for I had providently put the main wad in the upper left pocket of my shirt and no French thief ever would be smart enough to look in such a place for money. This *macquereau* got about six francs, and I got a nice lump on the side of my head, delivered, I believe, by a tire jack.

I hold no hatred for Lyon, for the police and the hospital people were all very kind. One of the doctors gave me a drink of wine as he was stitching away. The next morning my opinion of the city went higher, for at breakfast I had some of the famous sausage that is constructed there.

Sausage *lyonnais* is made from fresh pork—about five pounds —from which all the fat has been trimmed, chopped, and mixed with about a tablespoonful of salt and one teaspoonful of pepper. The butchers of Lyon then haul out a piece of pork fat which they have been salting until it has turned as dry as a long-dead starfish. They chop it up into quarter-inch cubes and add it to the chopped pork.

To this mixture is added a couple of good-sized garlic cloves, put through a press or smashed with the ever-popular cleaver, and about eight or ten white peppercorns. If you cannot get whole white peppercorns, use ground white pepper—but I doubt that you will not be able to find whole white ones in these days of plenty. Manganaro's, Ninth Avenue, New York, is a good source of peppercorns. Those lads have everything.

103

Get some huge hog bung from the butcher. Tie up one end and stuff into it this Lyon sausage, which you have mixed until your arms have begun to feel like those of a guard standing outside The Presidio in San Francisco, the place where old generals go. One bung should hold eight or ten pounds of sausage, provided its overall length is ten or twelve feet. Tie it all off into links of whatever size you wish. The incomparable *Larousse*, in speaking of Lyon sausage, recommends eighteen-inch lengths. This is too long, I assert. Eight or ten inches is quite long enough.

These sausages, after being tied up, should be hung up in a cool, dry place and left there for at least four days. Take them out and get a roll of string. Wrap them up and down and around and around and around, so that they will not curve. The idea is to get them all as straight as they can be, for they now face a drying process, in that same cool and dry place, that will go on for three, four or five months. They will keep beyond five months, but your teeth may not if you try biting into a five-monther.

Many of the good people of Lyon (my mugger is not included in that blanketing sentence) have been known to add well-cut beef, with all the fat removed, to their sausage. To me, this is not as good as the pure pork kind. It does hurry the sausage's drying, but it harms the taste.

Mostly, Lyon sausage is eaten cold, either on a platter with other cold meats or as an accompaniment to cocktails. It may be boiled or broiled. If the latter is essayed, it is well to put it on top of an English muffin (not the whole thing, just slices), with either Cheddar or Gouda cheese, sliced thinly, atop it.

When I serve it cold, I add some Westphalian ham, some Lebanon bologna, one or two slivers of dried beef, and perhaps some *leberwurst mit speck,* or just some plain *leberwurst.* Raw onions or scallions should be served with this platter. Small radishes. A stalk or two of celery. Green and black olives. Perhaps some pickles.

When I serve it hot, I add some steamed string beans to which some crushed walnuts have been added. Crushed salted peanuts also go happily with the steamed beans.

104

MEUSER MEAT LOAF. This is a Winchester Farm sausage recipe, and I must confess I do not know why it is called Meuser Meat Loaf. Perhaps there was some butcher named Meuser who either made the sausage or whose wife invented this meat loaf.

To make Meuser Meat Loaf, you first take about one-half pound of loose sausage which you mix with one whole pound of ground beef. I would choose chuck, if I were you. Round steak is much too expensive and ground sirloin is out of reason.

The sausage and the beef should be mixed together with one-half cup of finely chopped onion. Then add about twelve or thirteen or fourteen small soda crackers which you have previously pulverized in your pestle and mortar or crumbled cruelly with your massive hands. Salt and pepper, to taste, now go in. About a teaspoonful of salt, I should think, and about half that quantity of pepper.

Mix all these things well, either with your hands or with a wooden spoon. Toward the end of the mixing, pour in one-half cup of either ketchup or catsup, whatever its manufacturer calls it.

Work in the tomato sauce with either hands or wooden spoon, and put the whole mess in the kind of tin in which you might put a loaf of bread. Garnish the top with slices of onion which have been dipped in oil, and with chopped parsley that has been treated the same way. The top also might be sprinkled, again, very lightly, with salt and pepper.

That is all you have to do to this Meuser Meat Loaf. It now goes into the oven, which has been set to 350°. The Winchester Farm people say you ought to keep it there for an hour, but they are wrong. It ought to be kept in the oven for at least an hour and a half. If it seems to be getting too dry, baste it considerately with some stock made from a beef bouillon cube and some hot water, but not too liberally, please. Just enough to keep it fairly moist.

Some people have been known to put thin-sliced olives, stuffed with pimentoes, in this meat loaf. But do not use more than about a dozen, please.

This sausage—that is all it is, really, except that it is not prepared in any casing other than the metal pan—is best served with mashed potatoes, or Cope's corn, or fresh peas, or even canned peas. There ought to be some kind of jelly on the table—currant, strawberry, blackberry or gooseberry.

Try not to make the portions too generous when you first haul it steaming out of the oven. The best taste comes the next day, when the Meuser Meat Loaf is served cold in sandwiches, between thick slices of bread which have been spread with generous amounts of salt butter and fairly assertive prepared mustard. Such sandwiches are best accompanied by raw tomato and onion slices, and perhaps some black olives or some Fanning's bread-and-butter pickles.

MISS CAROL'S SAUSAGE CONCOCTION. This recipe comes to me through the courtesy of *The Southern Cook Book*, edited by Marion Brown, published originally by The University of North Carolina Press. Miss Carol is Miss Carol Hampton, who first published this recipe in *The Alexandria Woman's Club's Cook Book*, one of those marvelous club cookbooks that seem to be published somewhere every month of the year by women around the country.

Like so many of the recipes in here, this one requires work. A good deal of it. For one thing, there is the basic dish. For the other, there is the sauce. I have no idea of the identity of Miss Carol Hampton, but I am sure she is a superb cook. Here is how her sausage concoction is made.

Put about six slices of dried bread in a baking dish. Butter or grease it. (The dish, not the bread.) Now fry six cakes of sausage about the size of the average hamburger. I don't know, actually, how big the "average" hamburger is, but I imagine it is a little bigger than the one at the average White Tower. These sausage patties should be fried until they are slightly browned. They should be arranged over the bread.

While they are browning, slice an onion into six thick rounds. Make six rounds of cold mashed potatoes and put them into a frying pan and brown them. Put each onion round on top of each piece of sausage-and-bread and top each with a potato round.

All this goes into the baking pan, of course, and now comes the heavy work—what my old Army friends would have called "the hard duty." A sauce is now required, says Miss Carol. God help us all.

According to her rule, you take the drippings from the sausage you have just fried, add one-quarter cupful of cooking oil (she does not specify what kind), and one tablespoonful of diced salt pork. In my view, this is not enough. I should say one-half cupful. Dice and consign to this one clove of garlic, two tablespoonfuls of minced parsley, and about six fresh tomatoes, plus one-half of a chopped green pepper.

On top of this, put one-and-one-half teaspoonfuls of sage, one-half teaspoonful of thyme, and one-and-one-half teaspoonfuls of basil, along with six peppercorns which have been crushed either in your grinder or in a mortar. If you need, or desire, or just have a whim for, a very hot sauce, dried red peppers can be used. Only three, or you will run screaming from whatever shack you are cooking this in.

Cook all this for about one and one-half hours, stirring it all the while. Then pour over sausage *et al.* "Leftover lentils, green beans, peas, baked beans, may be added last five minutes," says Miss Carol Hampton.

She does not add how long the bread, sausage, potato and onion slices and sauce should be cooked together once they are in the fire, but I imagine that one-and-one-half hours in a 250° oven would be enough. This would give the dish three hours in all, and would enable the various ingredients to get on with each other in complete compatibility.

MUSTARD SAUCE AND SAUSAGE. Ah there, Mrs. Ruth Luecke! Where in the name of God do you get Russian sausage in Lancaster county, where you live? Leave that question unanswered, please. Just give me the recipe. So I wrote, and so this lady replied:

"Russian sausages, two per person. Skin them and slice them fine, and fry slowly in butter or table fat." (I think she means bacon grease or lard.) "Stir in two tablespoonfuls of flour, gradually add two cupfuls of milk, and simmer for about ten minutes." In a good iron skillet.

Then she says: "Prepared mustard." She does not say how much. All she says is, "Add prepared mustard until sauce is of desired sharpness."

It is impolite of me to disagree with the ladies who have contributed so many recipes to this book, but if I were called upon to say how to make this dish, I would call for Colman's mustard, the dry kind, and I would mix up—in water—about a tablespoonful of it. Colman's is as hot as it is possible for mustard to be, and this dish, made with Russian or American sausages, needs the tongue-quivering heat of this marvelous rubefacient.

Braised endive is good served on the side of this or, if it is springtime, dandelion greens, or some spinach or poke stems. If it is spinach, do the traditional recipe: about one-half a cup of vinegar, almost the same amount of sugar, both mixed well, and then four or five slices of crisp, crumbled bacon mixed in. I must warn you that this is a tough one to do properly. My mother has told me how to do it roughly five hundred times, and I still cannot do it the way she does.

Some people of German extraction recommend adding some dried apples, called *schnitz*, to the recipe. For some of the others in here, I would shout an affirmative. But for this mustard sauce recipe, I must demur. No apples, please. Sometimes the simplest recipes are the hardest to do, and they should not be given things they do not need. The closest I have come to interfering with this one is recommending the dry mustard treatment, and I rest with that.

OMELETTE WITH SAUSAGE. Put about one-half pound of loose sausage into the skillet for browning. Meanwhile, break six eggs into a bowl, rained on by two tablespoonfuls of water from the sink tap. Some people use milk in an omelette. Water is better. A chef in Paris told me that, and he was right. Next, one-half teaspoonful of salt goes in. Then, about one-half teaspoonful of onion salt. Finely chopped onion —*very* finely chopped—makes it even better.

Whisk the eggs and put in a small sprig or two of chopped parsley, a dash of Tabasco, and pour them over the sausage— first pouring some of the sausage grease into what I often refer to as my greasetainer.

If you haven't got an iron skillet, use a Corningware baking dish or some sort of baking pan. Place the receptacle in a 350° oven fifteen or twenty minutes, or until its contents are light and browned.

The wonderful thing about this omelette is that you don't have to turn it as you do the French kind. It lies there and behaves itself. It will do so even if you insist upon adding a dash of milk or possibly half milk and half water. When the omelette is taken out, it should be sprinkled with either cayenne or red pepper and garnished with parsley.

This is an excellent breakfast dish and is enhanced by the addition of quick-toast waffles on the side or just plain old buttered toast or some thick French bread cut into slices and buttered and done on the shelf of the oven above the omelette.

OXFORD HORNS. Said my late friend Gerald Kersh: Mince one pound of pork and shred one pound of suet. Mix with a half tablespoonful of sage, pinches of thyme, marjoram, lemon peel, nutmeg, salt and pepper as you wish it, and one gently beaten egg. "Make them into the long shapes of sausages," says Kersh, "and fry or grill."

OYSTER AND SAUSAGE LOAF. This recipe, so far as I know, originated at the famous Toll House near Whitman, Massachusetts. Presumably, it goes back to the time of the Puritans and Indians, but I am not enough of a culinary historian to make an assertive statement.

Combine one pound of sausage meat, one quart of raw oysters, a cup of bread crumbs, and two gently beaten eggs. Put them in a bread pan, meat loaf style, and bake at 350° for, oh, about an hour. Every once in a while, you should haul the pan out of the oven and get rid of the excess fat—of which there will be plenty.

The Toll House recommends serving this with hot Hollandaise Sauce. This is nonsense. The loaf should be served with a nice roux made from the oyster liquor, some of the sausage grease, butter, milk, a pinch of parsley, and enough cornstarch to thicken it. Sliced black olives should be added.

Another sausage-oyster thing you might try is even easier. Parboil the sausages, then poke them and let their own grease cook them, or add a little butter or oil. When they are browned, remove them to a covered pan and put the pan in the oven.

Now, while the sausages are in the oven awaiting their ultimate fate, consign the oysters to theirs. Drain off all but about a tablespoonful of the fat the sausage has cooked in. Take about three tablespoonfuls of the oyster liquor and spoon it over the sausages while they are warming in the oven.

If you are serving four people, you ought to have bargained for at least six oysters per person. Now pop those oysters into sizzling, angry sausage fat. Squeeze the juice of half a lemon or lime over them. If you like sweetish things, you may use the juice of half a very juicy orange. Or of a red meat grapefruit. Remember this: no oyster should ever be sizzled for more than two minutes on either side.

Some people like to pop these oysters into breadcrumbs before putting them into the pan, coating them thoroughly. I feel this is not gilding the lily, but bronzing it. They are perfectly fine as they come snarling up from the pan, a little brown, and ready to join their sausage brothers in their last march down into your stomach.

Cut up the sausage before serving. Make them into a series of coins about one-half-inch thick. Turn off the oven and put both sausages and oysters into it to introduce themselves to each other. You might squeeze some more lemon, lime, or orange juice over these new bedmates, although not too much. I have to confess that I do not know how much "too much" is. You might also add some of the green parts of cut-up scallions.

Now, make a gravy from the grease etc., brown bits, remnants of oysters, etc., left in the pan. Do not use milk. Use water and what may be left of the oyster liquor, plus flour or cornstarch. Whisk it well and put in some celery salt, garlic powder, monosodium glutamate and a pinch of gumbo file powder. I sometimes add a pinch or two of dry mustard to this overpowering combination although it is not necessary.

Take out the plates. Put a portion of sausage and another of oysters on each one. Pour the gravy you have just conquered over them. On the side, put several other things such as bread and butter pickles, or Major Grey's, or grits or mashed potatoes. Under no circumstances should you ever use fried potatoes. A salad will do.

You do not need the large Saddle Rocks for this recipe. The smaller Baltimore oysters will do. And, if you happen to live in the northwestern states, so will Olympics.

ARISIAN SAUCISSON.   Made from the same meat as Lyon sausage but seasoned a bit differently.

Into the pork go two tablespoonfuls of salt for each two pounds, plus one teaspoonful of freshly ground black pepper, one-half teaspoonful of pounded pimento, and a very small amount—two pinches—of saltpeter.

This should be stuffed into pork intestines and tied in eight-inch lengths and hung up to dry. Also known as *cervelat*, this sausage is most often steeped first in just-boiled water, then taken out and sautéed gently in butter.

A variation of this is to make *saucisson-cervelat ordinaire.* Using the same amount of salt and pepper for each two pounds of pork, and a couple of pinches of saltpeter, this sausage consists mainly of coarsely chopped pork, including ears and shins and feet, plus pork fat.

This mixture is put into beef casings, tied off at eight or twelve inches, and smoked. Some say it should be smoked lightly. Others insist that it should be left in the smokehouse for days. I think one day in a smokehouse is enough for any sausage.

PARTRIDGE SAUSAGES.   The sausage made from partridge is seldom made in this country. It is a great favorite in France and *Mitteleurope*, where it is known as *Königswurste*, or Sausage for the King.

Six or seven partridges are first poached and then boned. The same process can be applied to two small chickens, the fatter the better. Cornish hens will do. The boned fowl is ground together once, then again.

This sausage is not inexpensive. Minced truffles are added to the poultry mixture—about one-half cupful of them. Then a cupful of chopped mushrooms. Two eggs are beaten lightly and poured in. Then some fine Rhine wine is added. The idea is to get the sausage stiff—but not too stiff. Into the chopped-up bird mixture go salt, coarsely ground pepper, and one-quarter teaspoonful of mace. Still more mixing is needed.

This sausage should be stuffed into a fairly large pig bung and then tied off at intervals of five or six inches. It should be poached and served hot, or allowed to cool and then sliced and served cold. I prefer the hot way. Cope's corn is good on the side of this sausage. Or boiled potatoes with black butter.

The warning that goes with this sausage: do not fry or sauté it. You will kill the flavor of the game.

PENNSYLVANIA DUTCH SAUSAGE PIE. Has it dawned on any of my readers that I come from the Pennsylvania Dutch country? Well, I do, and, not only am I proud of it, but rather defiant about it. Many of the wild recipes in this book came from down Lancaster way. The housewives in that area were most gracious in sending along their own special rules, as the persevering reader will have found out if he or she has had the fortitude to come along this far. One of the best recipes is this one for a pie.

In salted water, boil about one and one half pounds of potatoes which have been cut in chunks. Good big chunks. I like to cook them scrubbed but unpeeled, for the earthy taste of the skin. While they are cooking on the stove, I take some pie crust dough and line a pie tin with it, reserving some of the dough for the topping.

Into the pie, I cram as many uncooked small sausages as I can—usually about twelve or fourteen. They get sprinkled with parsley and a small pinch of freshly ground pepper. The potatoes go over the sausage when they're almost soft enough to eat, and peeled. The lady who sent me this, Mrs. Roy Wittle, suggests sprinkling a few drops of water over the mixture before the lid of crust is set on.

Mrs. Wittle bakes this pie for fifteen minutes in a 450° oven, then turns it back to 325° and keeps it in that heat for about thirty minutes. The topping should be brushed with butter before the pie is set into the oven.

PEPPERS STUFFED WITH SAUSAGE. The night before I went off to the Army, my mother gave me stuffed peppers. I could not eat them again for about twenty years, for they all came up the next morning. This, I believe, was due more to my emotions and reluctance than to the peppers. Now that nearly three decades have fallen off the calendar, I have been able to eat stuffed peppers again, and one of the best and easiest ways I know of making them is with sausages.

Get a lot of large green or red or green-and-red peppers. Two for each guest. Cut off and save their tops and scrape out their seeds. Run some water into each pepper to clean out any seeds that cling.

Now fry some loose sausage meat, permitting the grease to remain in the pot or skillet or spider or whatever you are using. Add to the sausage an equal volume of bread crumbs, a few cut up mushrooms, and some chopped celery. Mix it all well and use it for stuffing the peppers.

Replace the tops and set the stuffed peppers in a pan with about one-half teaspoonful of water. Put the pan in the oven, which should be going at about 300°. Go and shoot yourself a couple of games of eight-ball, just to keep your eye keen and your senses generally on the alert. Sniff occasionally, and go in and baste the peppers every once in a while. They should cook for about one and a half hours.

Inevitably, if you serve these stuffed peppers, there will be those who claim their mothers made them in a way they will never forget. Ignore them.

PIG BELLY, A NEW WAY. *Metzelsuppe*, or pig belly, or hog maw, or pig's stomach, is one recipe I swore I would never write down again. I had already done it in three cookbooks.

Then, in the spring of 1967, a lady named Mrs. Willis L. Shopf, Jr., of Millersville, Pennsylvania, sent me a recipe which she entitled, "The *new way* taste for the old favorite PIG STOMACH." Since pig's stomach, or pig belly, is really at heart, or at stomach, a sausage, I feel I had better include this one. It differs from the rules of my mother and my aunts, but it is worth recording.

Mrs. Schopf gets a pig's stomach from her butcher and washes it inside and out. She gets two pounds of loose sausage. If she can't get that, she strips the casing off two pounds of link sausage. She peels and coarsely dices four or five cupfuls of potatoes. Now she attacks an onion and gives that the chopping business. Next she goes after two stalks of celery, chopping both. Setting the sausage aside, she puts all the vegetables in a stew pot and covers them with water, letting them stew until the potatoes are just about soft.

Meanwhile, she is either cutting up stale bread or warming some bread in the oven to make it as stiff as a Columbia, Pennsylvania, drunk on a Saturday night. To the bread, which she has cut into cubes, she adds her sausage meat. She has already taken her vegetables off the stove and drained them.

This all sounds like a lot to do, but it should be remembered that most Lancaster County housewives lost their right hands to sausage grinders when they were very small. Now, she puts in the vegetables. She mixes the sausage, bread and vegetables with her hands, meanwhile singing a chorus of *Wonderful Good*. "Mix good and fill stomach," she tells me. "Sew opening or just use skewers."

Once she has got the belly tightly secured, she puts it on a rack in the oven and keeps it there until it has cooked at 300° for one-and-one-half to two hours. During this time, I think she sits down and reads a copy of the *Sunday News* to find out who has died. One of the principal hobbies of Lancaster County ladies is going to funerals, whether or not they knew the deceased. She is also basting the sausage with its own grease once every fifteen minutes.

"Stick with sharp fork several times to allow grease to run out," Mrs. Schopf writes me. "Slice and serve."

Slice and serve, all right, if you can wrestle this behemoth

115

out of the oven. If you are not extremely careful, it may try to fight you. I recommend two forks and another human being who is armed with a large spatula. The stomach should be browned by this time.

In all the years I have been eating pig belly, I always have had it boiled. The belly itself has never tasted good to me. It has always been like trying to bite into one of those old tires the boy with the candle never managed to lug home in his winsome nightshirt. One can eat pickled tripe, head cheese, or pork sausage by the ton, but it is too much to ask of a man to eat the outer casing of pig belly when it has simply been boiled. Mrs. Willis L. Schopf, Jr., seems to have found the way to circumvent this and I am grateful to her for having sent along her recipe.

PILAFF OF SAUSAGE. No, I never ate this in any of the countries where they ordinarily serve pilaff. Not in Russia, not in Turkey, not in Greece. Nor do I ever want to eat it in those countries where there are too many flies and beggers for me at my age. But I do like it and eat it here.

Take as many sausages as you think you will need and broil or fry them lightly. While they are getting done, boil water for rice, the quick or slow kind—I prefer the latter unless I am pressed for time. There isn't much difference, anyhow.

Put two bouillon cubes in the water. Also sauté an onion about the circumference of a lady's compact. Do not use salt in this dish. When the sausages are done, throw them into the boiling water. Also throw in half a cup of rice for each cup of boiling water. Also throw in the sautéed onions. The whole thing is baked in a 400° oven for about twenty minutes or until the stock is just about used up. Keep an eye on the dish as it is working away in the oven. Burned pilaff is not really much good.

The top of the dish may be sprinkled with sliced almonds or pine nuts or English walnuts. Another variation is to put Parmesan or Romano cheese—grated, how else?—on it.

It can also be made into a kind of curry in which you first

116

brown the rice in about two tablespoonfuls of oil—the more exotic the better—and one-and-one-half tablespoonfuls of onion. Add the curry powder and then do the rice the regular way and add the sausage. Saffron may be substituted for the curry powder, although I find that this gives the sausage a greenish tinge.

One final variation is to use loose sausage or very small pieces of cut-up links. Mix the meat well with cooked rice, adding some curry powder—but not much—and then roll this mixture up in grape leaves.

This is the Greek-Armenian-Turkish method. After the tied-up grape leaves have been sautéed in olive oil for a short time, more stock should be added to the baking dish in which the sautéed and stuffed leaves are transported for baking for about 45 minutes at 300°.

Sausage pilaff can also be served in eggplant halves which have had the pulp scooped out, then brushed with oil and broiled for about twenty minutes. Or in scooped-out zucchini or tomatoes.

PINEAPPLE AND SAUSAGE CAKES. "Pineapple and sausage?" I questioned a lady I know. "Why certainly," she said, and forthwith prepared them, using Winchester Farm sausage patties.

This recipe is so simple that I believe my dachshund could make it by himself. First he would drain a can of chilled pineapple and rub the slices with either horseradish or mustard. Then, he would oil a flat baking dish. Into this would go the pineapple slices with a sausage cake on top of each one. He would bake these in a moderate oven—about 350°—for half an hour, basting them occasionally with the pineapple juice he drained from the can.

This dish gets served with a garnishing of parsley or chopped chives, fresh or frozen. It makes a fine breakfast or lunch.

POLENTA AND SAUSAGES. That great man and great art director, Nelson Gruppo, may be somewhat handicapped in doing his work because of this recipe. Polenta, which is made from Italian corn meal that can be found in any good or bad Italian grocery needs to be stirred constantly. It is hard on men's muscles.

I had had polenta at Gruppo's apartment a number of times and have seen him come to the table, after making it, white and trembling as though with the ague.

To make it, buy about a pound of polenta at your Italian grocery. Add about one-and-one-half cups of it to about six cups of tempestuously boiling water. Then, gradually add one-and-one-half cups more. Stir, stir, stir. Soon bubbles will begin to break on the surface. "Pouf!" the polenta will say, as though in contempt for you.

Meanwhile, be boiling anywhere from one-half to a pound of sausages. When the parboiling water is done for, permit them to brown for a bit in the same vessel.

By this time, the polenta will be done—and so will your arms. Take the wooden spoon with which you have been stirring and turn this accursed cornmeal into a shallow baking dish. Set it in either a draft or a refrigerator so that it cools off. The rest of this recipe, now that you have given your arms a lifelong constriction of the muscles, is relatively simple.

While the polenta is cooling, cut up the browned sausages and grease a good-sized casserole, using some sort of vegetable oil or butter. Then cut up the cooled-off polenta into one-inch squares. Put the sausage and polenta into the casserole, alternating them layer by layer. The polenta will probably come out on top. Sprinkle it lavishly with grated cheese.

Now add this sauce, which is simplicity itself. Cook together, until they are smooth, a tablespoonful of oil, a tablespoonful of flour, and one-half cup of beef stock. Simmer in this about two pounds of well cut up peeled tomatoes, two minced onions, a bayleaf, a pinch of either oregano or thyme, two whole cloves, and a half cup of chopped parsley. Simmer until the mixture is thick and then add a small piece of butter about the size of two Las Vegas dice pasted together.

Pour this mixture all over the polenta and sausage. It will have the effect of sinking the cheese, sending it all through the

118

casserole. Put more cheese on the top and cook it in the oven at 350° for at least an hour—although, if I were calling time on this one, I would say an hour-and-a-half.

At the end, one cup of dry white wine should be cascaded in and this lovely mixture should be permitted to heat through again. The wine is not necessary—it just improves the whole thing, and if you are as addicted to wine cookery as I am, you will be glad you did it.

A variation on this is to add a layer of zucchini between layers of the sausage and polenta—or two layers, or three, depending upon how much you have cooked and how many people are coming to dinner. The zucchini should not be fried. It should be boiled until it is soft enough to be fork-poked, and then it should be either coined or cut lengthwise into slender strips. Do not add onion rings. There is enough onion in the sauce. There probably will not be enough of this dish to go around, but thank the Lord for that. It is not one of those dishes that tastes better the next day.

One more ingredient is necessary. Keep a bottle of linament nearby to sooth your aching arms.

PONED SAUSAGES. Mrs. R. Theodore Bixler, the sister-in-law of an old boyhood friend of mine, Clifford Hilton, sent me this fine and ridiculously easy recipe.

Brown as many sausages as you believe you will need. Lightly, if you please. Take one package of Jim Dandy corn muffin mix and do what it says to do on the package—*i.c.*, preheat the oven to 450°, combine one cup of milk and two tablespoonfuls of shortening, and add the contents of the corn muffin mix. Stir all together.

Grease a deep circular baking pan. On the bottom of it, put the browned sausages. Cover them with the batter and bake for around twenty to twenty-five minutes, or until the top of the mix is golden brown.

I wonder if Clifford Hilton is still listening to those old Glenn Miller 78s we collected more than thirty years ago?

119

PORK BRAINS SAUSAGE.   Called *Gehirnwurste* in German, and *Saucisses de Cervelle* in French, and practically nothing in the United States because they are rarely seen here except in limited localities, pork brains sausage may be made at home. If the cook's stomach stays with him, they may be eaten with some enjoyment.

Pork brains are first cooked in a brine of about two tablespoonfuls of salt to a quart of water, then ground up with their equal in pork meat, half fat, half lean. The meat is seasoned with mace and salt and pepper and forced into pork bung which then is tied together in six-inch sections. Tie them at the ends, and, if you wish, put knots between each section.

The sections should be poached or steamed for about seven or eight minutes in boiling water—not much of it—that looks as though it could take on Vesuvius. When the water is boiled away, the sausages should be allowed to lie there in their pan and act as though they are angry about the removal of their maternal water. You, meanwhile, will have pricked them so that their juices will enable them to brown. Turn them two or three times with a wooden fork. Serve them with lightly sautéed onions and tomatoes, lightly sprinkled with grated green pepper.

Gehirnwurste is more German than French and so is generally served with sauerkraut. In France, it is usually accompanied by beans. In the southern part of the U.S., where there are small German neighborhoods, it is set forth with Jim Dandy grits or cornbread. In St. Louis and Cincinnati, where there are large German colonies, the people will give you mashed potatoes with this item. On the west coast, they may give you a pineapple banana split. Set it aside.

An excellent gravy may be made from the drippings from this pan in the usual manner—water and flour, monosodium glutamate, salt and pepper, and not more than a capful of Kitchen Bouquet. This is good only if served with grits or mashed potatoes. It is not good with banana splits or oranges.

POT PIE WITH SAUSAGE.   This is not really a pie. It is

what the Pennsylvania Dutch call "bot boi," and it is more like a stew. My mother used to make it with chicken and sometimes with beef or pork. It can be done with sausage. (If it couldn't, what would it be doing in this book?) The recipe was sent to me by Mrs. Nelson White of Paradise, Pennsylvania, who evidently is an excellent cook.

"My mother and father made sausage," Mrs. White wrote to me. "My husband and I make it, and we have helped our son make it. We think ours is good, and we hope you do, too."

Then, she got to her basic sausage rule: "First, keep all the meat clean." She did not specify how much meat to use. I would judge it to be between six and eight pounds.

"You take all the choice trimmings from the hams and shoulders, the backbones and the neck meat. You can also cut up a shoulder if you want more. Cut up all the meat into small slices or pieces about an inch square, and feed it very slowly into a meat grinder. This meat should be as lean as possible. Grind up all of this real fine, add at least two cups of salt and a handful of the *freshest* pepper you can get, a handful of brown sugar and a teaspoonful of saltpeter. Now you mix all this together, with clean hands is the best. It takes a lot of mixing."

Out of her sausage, Mrs. White makes what Lancaster Countians call Sausage Pot Pie. "First, cook potatoes, enough for family," she said in her letter. (I think this means one large potato for each person who is to be served.)

"Cook potatoes in salted water twenty minutes and add your sausage." About two three-and-one-half-inch links for each person, I would think, except if you are using Jones's sausages, in which case you will need at least three links per person. "Add a half-bottle of Heinz ketchup," Mrs. White said. "No more water, also dash of pepper."

Then she said: "Start to make your pot pie dough." But, alas, she did not tell me how. My mother did, though, over the telephone. All doughs terrify me. The ones I have made over the years could have been rolled into projectiles and fired from howitzers, or filled with TNT and dropped from helicopters.

My mother's recipe for *bot boi* dough goes as follows: "Beat two eggs in a bowl. Add four half-eggshells of water. Salt this, but not with too much salt. Add one-and-one-half teaspoonfuls of baking powder and enough flour to make the whole mixture stiff. Flour a board and roll out this paste. Permit it to stand for about two hours, turning it once in a while. Then cut it into slices or squares, depending on how you like it."

Now Mrs. White's letter cuts in again: "Drop the dough on top of the cooking sausage and potatoes in the pot. Keep cooking with the lid on. After each addition of dough, add a little water and loosen the dough, one piece from another, so it cooks slowly and evenly. Continue this until all the dough is in the pot and top it all with sprigs of parsley and a dash of pepper."

And sit yourself down for an excellent meal.

There is one fault I would find with Mrs. White's excellent *bot boi*. I would add a couple of chicken bouillon cubes to the stock. I might even add three or four chicken wings.

On the side, there ought to be either coleslaw, or steamed broccoli, or steamed spinach, or all three.

POTATO SALAD AND SAUSAGE. Bertha E. L. Stockbridge of Riverside, Illinois, must have been a marvelous woman and a superb cook. In 1922, she published a fine book called *The Practical Cookbook*. There was no nonsense about it. Every recipe was delineated clearly and there were a few hints on home nostrums and cures as well.

One of Bertha's best recipes was for potato salad and sausage, as follows. Cut however much sausage you feel will be needed into what she calls "tiny pieces." About a cupful, she recommends. To this should be added two cupfuls of chopped potatoes, one finely-diced pickled beet, about a teaspoonful of parsley, and a small grated onion. This should be mixed with mayonnaise and served on lettuce.

Bertha neglected to preface her rule by saying that the sausage should be cooked beforehand. Cooks are often careless that way. They have their minds set so hard on their work that they often forget details when giving recipes.

POTATO SAUSAGE CASSEROLE. While Mrs. Suzanne C. Hartman of Martha Avenue, Lancaster, tells me that "pig stomachs are hard to come by these days," I don't agree. In order to make her recipe, she should go to Central Market in Lancaster, where pig stomachs are as easy to come by as radishes in spring, or to S. Clyde Weaver, or some other country butchers. People outside the Pennsylvania Dutch area should beware of recipes for pig belly or stomach or "hog maw" as it is called in that area. Except in Berks, Montgomery and Lancaster counties, they really are hard to come by.

This is a passable substitute.

To one pound of loose sausage, add five medium-sized potatoes, one small chopped onion, one quarter of a teaspoon of oregano, and salt and pepper to taste.

The sausage should be precooked in about one half cupful of water for about fifteen minutes. "Break the sausage with a fork as it cooks," wrote Mrs. Hartman to me. "Drain off excess fat. Combine all the other ingredients with the sausage and turn into a one-and-one-half quart casserole. Cover it and bake it in a 325° oven about one hour, or until the potatoes are tender."

This sounds good, but I would add more onion and some parsley, as well as about one half a head of pre-boiled cabbage, boiled with some carroway seeds. Not too much, please. Some pieces of dry bread, soaked in water or milk, also go well in this dish.

POTATO SAUSAGE LOAF. Mrs. Herman Erickson of Wahoo, Nebraska, gave this recipe to the *Nebraska Centennial First Ladies' Cookbook*, and a splendid rule it is. It came originally from Sweden.

"The pioneer women prepared food from recipes which they brought with them and observed many of the traditions of their homeland," Mrs. Erickson writes. She was born in Nebraska, but her ties to Sweden are still strong.

The recipe is forbiddingly heavy, but I have tried it and it is excellent. Take one onion and put it through the meat grinder with enough raw, peeled potatoes to make about one pint. Get one pound of ground chuck and one-half pound of ground fresh pork. Mix them with the potato-onion grindings plus one teaspoonful of allspice and one of pepper and salt to taste. Some people might want to add a beaten egg, but I don't think it is necessary. Put all this in a casserole or bread pan and bake for about an hour or a little longer at 350°.

Instead of fresh pork, veal may be used. Or ground-up chicken. The beauty of this recipe is its simplicity.

POTATOES AND SMOKED SAUSAGE. A fine old lady I know, Anna Kready, aged 86, sent me this recipe. I am going to reprint it exactly as she wrote it, for she may be a distant relative of mine, and it is dangerous to get into trouble with relatives. Here goes Anna Kready:

"Take one pound of smoked sausages, cut into about two-inch pieces, add a small onion cut fine, put in a skillet, simmer for an hour (at least), and then let the juice dry up and brown the sausage. Take six or more good-sized potatoes and cut them up (not too fine). Add the potatoes to the sausage, cover with water, boil until the taters are good and soft. Serve piping hot."

POTATOES WITH SAUSAGE. This is similar to the recipe for Apples and Sausages.

All you do is peel as many large potatoes as you think you will need, make a hole through the middle of each one with an apple corer or some other good stout tool, take out the cored part, chop it fine, mix it with sausage meat, and stuff the mixture back into the potatoes. An old-fashioned clothespin works well for this endeavor.

The potatoes should be salted and peppered and put into a good roasting pan with about a half-inch of water, and then baked for about an hour or a little more, at 350°. Cut-up link sausages may be substituted for the loose meat.

There is only one precaution; obviously, mashed potatoes should not be served on the side. Broccoli is good, or cauliflower, or perhaps asparagus or peas or, best of all, creamed onions.

POULTRY SAUSAGE. Making poultry sausage, which the French do so competently as a matter of course, was so puzzling to me that I finally gave up and waited patiently until work took me to Paris. Not only was it puzzling to make, but it was also puzzling to the local poulterers, who wondered why I wanted chicken or turkey intestines. They grudgingly would hand them over, charging roughly ten cents for three or four pounds.

I would take the bird bowels home and soak them in several changings of heavily salted water while I stewed a chicken for about two hours, along with a carrot and onion, poultry seasoning and salt and pepper.

Now I'll make the sausage, I always thought. And I was as wrong as I ever had been in my life. I minced the chicken, put it through the grinder with the finest blade, added some lemon juice, and a little olive oil, and a beaten egg, and put it through again. Finally, it was perfect. It was about the texture and consistency of the ham salad you can buy in Harry's, a superb delicatessen in New Canaan, Connecticut.

Then I tried to stuff the intestines with the boned and ground chicken mixture. It either refused to go in or the casings did not want it in. Both remained stubborn as an obdurate Amish youth being dragged to a wedding his father had arranged with a neighboring farmer's homely daughter.

Back I would go to Paris on another magazine assignment. There, in the *bistros* and the *boites*, would be those skinny, delicate chicken sausages, simmering on grilles.

"How do you stuff those sausage?" I asked a *boulanger*.

He was extremely cooperative. He shrugged. The second man I asked became excited and enraged. He thought I was trying to steal his secrets. He said he knew Americans, that they were as bad as Boche, and that I was wearing that beard to try to look French. I was not fooling him, he said. At one point, he turned to his assistant and ordered him to go for the neighborhood policeman. I skinned out of there and went up a side street.

I made no more inquiries after that.

The trouble with me is almost as puzzling as the trouble with making chicken sausage. Just as its flavor will not quit, as the jazz musicians say, I will not give up.

A friend of mine in London sent me a marrow spoon made during the reign of George VI. One day I was using it to scoop some marrow out of beef shin bones when the miraculous inspiration descended from Heaven into my earthbound brain. The spoon, with its wide end and smaller end, would be perfect for stuffing chicken intestines.

I went to the poultryman's place immediately and asked for some chicken intestines. "You again?" he asked. I more or less scuffed my foot, seized the intestines he sold me, bought a stewing chicken from him, and rushed home to plunge the intestines into a salty brine and the chicken into some boiling water. The poor marrow bones were still there on the counter, all but untouched. I scooped them all out and put the marrow in a small bowl.

When the chicken was done, I boned it and put it into the grinder, skin and all. Taking the marrow, I mixed it with the minced chicken meat and put it all through the grinder again. Then I took my George VI marrow spoon and took one of the chicken intestines by its open end and began cramming the marrow-and-chicken into it. It went in with extreme docility.

I tied this sausage off about every twelve inches, for it was only about three-quarters of an inch thick. The next question was—to smoke or not to smoke? I decided against smoking because I could not wait to taste it.

Putting about two tablespoonfuls of butter into the frying pan, I let it get sizzling hot, and then began putting in the chicken sausage in coils—tight coils, so that they would turn easily when I applied the spatula. They began to exude some juice of their own, and after about five minutes, I decided to let them have their own private execution and mercifully covered the pot.

This dish does not take long because the chicken casings brown easily and the chicken has already been cooked. About five minutes, covered, will do. Then take the pan off the fire, remove the cover, and give it to some child to wash. After you

126

have drained the pan, let the chicken sausage return to the stove and get *really* brown, at a lower heat.

Some people do not like marrow. But if you have anti-marrow people coming to dinner, it is still a good idea to use the marrow spoon just for stuffing the ground chicken into the intestines. It is the only implement that will enable you to make chicken sausage, no matter what the stuffing.

If, for some inscrutable reason, you are not fond of marrow, you can chop chicken livers which have been parboiled or sautéed—preferably the former—and then put them through the grinder along with the boned chicken parts and the hapless bird's heart and gizzard.

When you are about to remove this delicious sausage from the fire, douse it with a good stiff slug of brandy. You will have turned it once so that it is brown on both sides as you take it out.

The French serve sauerkraut with this *saucisson*. Sometimes they use it as an ingredient of *le grand choucroute*, along with hunks of pork and sausages of other kinds. I believe it to be better all by itself with, perhaps, some peas on the side. Or some mashed potatoes or grits.

Making it and stuffing it takes more trouble and bother than you may think it worth, but it is indeed worth it. And, I repeat, the marrow spoon is the only tool that will stuff chicken intestines.

PRETZELS AND SAUSAGE. This dish comes out of the sentimental memories of my Pennsylvania Dutch childhood.

One night, I was grilling some sausage links in a commonplace frying pan. I was about to make some mashed potatoes when I realized that I did not feel favorably inclined toward mashed potatoes that night. I do not know what kind of potatoes I *did* feel like; those still buried under the ground, I believe—for at that time I was midstream in a novel and not much interested in cooking.

I thought: Oh, hell, I'll open up a small can of stewed tomatoes and throw them in when the sausages are nearly done, and

127

then I'll add some sage and thyme or poultry seasoning, and a small bit of salt and some cayenne, and some monosodium glutamate, and I'll have myself a fine meal. (I often have long thoughts like that).

I began to think again. A small onion, I thought. A very small pepper, I also thought. I performed those acts, and had to admit to myself that it all tasted good. But not good enough.

About a month before, two friends who operate the Anderson Pretzel Bakery in Lancaster, Clarence Yohn and Donald Mc-Cullough, had given me a huge can of pretzels. I had kept them tightly closed in the can, so they were still fresh and crisp.

On pure, star-crazed impulse, I bit into one and knew my intuition was correct. I grabbed a handful of pretzels, wrapped my other hand around them, and crushed one pretzel against another. While the sausage and the stewed tomatoes and the onion and the pepper were all engaged in a wild dance with the various herbs in the pan, I set the pretzel bits aside until I was certain the sausages and their sauce were done.

This was reckless. I could not be certain that I was doing a sensible thing. After a while, I tasted the sauce. It was excellent. I was delighted that I had decided to put the poultry seasoning in with the other herbs. I took my crushed-up pretzels, hurled them on the sausages and sauce, and let them lie there for about forty seconds. Then I took the whole mess off the stove, garnished the dish lightly with fresh parsley sprigs, and served it up. The pretzels had stayed crisp. They blended perfectly with the sausages. It was as though the two had been made for each other.

The late Alex Tisdale, Cherry Lane Farm, Pottstown, Pennsylvania, was the man behind the National Pretzel Institute. He and his wife Marie, who used to wear a cloth pretzel on her hat, advocated pretzel stuffing for various fowl. Pretzel stuffing, as in the following recipe, is usually made with sausage.

Get a capon, small turkey, guinea, goose, or plain old barnyard rooster, and rub the bird inside and out with salt and pepper. In a bowl, mix some chopped onion, a stalk or two of chopped celery, and a cut-up green pepper. Sprinkle all this

128

with about three-quarters of a tablespoonful of poultry seasoning and one tablespoonful of poppy seeds. Mix it as hard as you
can. Break one egg into a bowl, along with two ounces of milk,
and whisk it. Pour that into the other ingredients. Also, mix in
about a half-pound of loose sausage, one-quarter of a pound of
ground veal or beef, and a can of water chestnuts which have
been smashed up with a cleaver. Mix everything together with
your hands.

Now wreak havoc on your Anderson pretzels with your
hands, about six inches above the bowl of stuffing-to-be. Grind
four or five in that handful. Be as merciless as the lions were
to the Christians.

Again, with your hands, mix the pretzels into the stuffing.
Sprinkle it with paprika and mix it one more time. Grind in
about three turns of the pepper mill. Get out a head of lettuce
—iceburg is best, but romaine or endive will do—and mix in a
handful of lettuce slivers, small ones, into the stuffing.

Pry loose all the bird's yellow fat, stuff the bird, and truss it.
Render the fat and pour it into another pan along with about
a cupful of dry white wine or cider. Put a bay leaf into this, a
very small onion, or two or three cleaned scallions, one carefully washed leek, and a chopped carrot. Add one cup of water
and a chicken bouillon cube for this basting fluid you are making. Go easy on salt; the pretzels will provide salt enough. But
dash in some salt and pepper.

Start the trussed gentleman at 400°, and after about fifteen
minutes, turn the oven down to 350°. Baste the bird every fifteen or twenty minutes; this will impart a rich brown crust to
the skin.

"What are we going to do with the giblets?" the housewife
will now cry. Put the gizzard and heart into the basting fluid in
the roasting pan. At about one-half hour before the bird is done,
add the liver. Chop the gizzard and heart in mid-cooking. Chop
the liver before you throw it in. Take the remaining basting
fluid at the end, add some drippings from the pan, and make a
gravy with some flour or cornstarch.

If you have basted your bird properly and regularly, it will

129

not need carving. It will come apart at the sound of a child's voice in the next room. Or, in the words of Morton Thompson: "Speak harshly to it, and it will fall apart."

Afterthoughts. About one-half can of diced pineapple may be added to the stuffing, or about one tablespoonful of preserved ginger. One crushed clove can be added. If this is done, the sausage and pretzel stuffing can be used in duck, in which case, one-half cup of honey should be added to the basting fluid.

QUICK, EASY SAUSAGE STEW. A lady from Strasburg, Pennsylvania, sent me this recipe under the stipulation, "Do not use my name." All right, nameless lady, I won't use your name, but I will use the recipe here.

Cut about two pounds of smoked sausage into two-inch pieces. Quarter four or five potatoes, each the size of a twelve-year-old Amish boy's clenched fist. Get out one or two medium-sized cans of kidney beans. I suppose she means red ones, even though you could use white. The potatoes and sausages are put into a pot and covered with a quart of water and boiled until the potatoes are soft. Then add the beans, heat through, and serve.

Salt and pepper should be added by the companions of the festive board. I grant this dish a garnish of parsley, but it is not really necessary. There should be bread for the mop-up procedure and coleslaw on the side.

RATH. One of the best of the sausage purveyors that I know in the United States is Rath Packing Company, which makes bacon, plain pork sausage, and many other items. Its products are uniformly excellent, with no waste. At the plant, before they wrap the dry sausage up to ship it off, they cut off either end, so that the *wurst* goes into the slicer to be cut up at once.

An outstanding product is Rath Bung Bologna, which consists of fresh beef and pork, carefully blended, and chopped medium-fine. Rath gives out no secrets. I gather that this sausage is put into beef bung. I can never tell the difference between bung flavors of pork, beef, veal or lamb.

Another sure crowd-pleaser is Rath Jumbo Thuringer, made of beef, pork, and beef and pork hearts, seasoned with whole white peppers, German marjoram, and, the company says, "other spices." As with Bung Bologna, this is smoked for about as long as it would take to see a rerun of *Gone With The Wind*.

A third Rath winner is Regular Brechteen Hard Salami, consisting of lean pork and beef, loosely chopped, along with Rath's own Salami Seasoning. I imagine that this is ground black pepper, a bit of sage, and some other herbs which I confess I am unable to identify.

This sausage is hung in the drying room for 42 to 56 days. It shrinks by about 30 to 35 per cent, and gets so hard that a policeman could carry it as a night stick. Like the others, it is stuffed into an animal casing. "Bright, lasting color is achieved by holding the product 24 to 48 hours in a high humidity curing room," says the company. Then, they add, they put it in the smokehouse for a time, usually for 36 to 48 hours.

One of the few sausages the Rath folk make in artificial cas-

132

ing in their spotless Aquila D'Oro kitchens is dried from 30 to 90 days. This, they say, is made "only from the lean hearts of picnics"—whatever that means. Butts, I imagine. Whole white peppers, garlic, "and other seasonings" are added to this eighteen-inch sausage.

Heavy Smoked Thuringer is another Rath favorite of mine. As with the Jumbo Smoked Thuringer, it is made of beef and pork and their hearts, to which whole white peppers and German marjoram are added. Also a few other herbs which Rath will not reveal. This has no garlic in it, damn it. But it is smoked for so long a time, you can imagine it wanting to break down the smokehouse doors. Probably for days. It emerges from the smokehouse and awaits its turn to be hung on hooks, where the hickory smoke fumes give it a rich, tangy flavor.

Whole black peppers are used in Rath's Cooked Salami, a mixture of pork and beef, chopped medium coarse, mixed with chopped garlic and other spices, and then placed together in artificial casing before being hung in smoke houses for God knows what length of time. Cooked salami is my least favorite, but many people eat it with sighs of passion.

Sicilian Salami is made primarily of pork trimmings and whole boneless picnic trimmings, chopped together coarsely. Both white and black peppers are added. All this is stuffed into a hog bung, smoked, and then hung in the drying room for five or six weeks.

Rath also makes a Genoa Salami which comes in bung, not artificial casing. This is also pork, beef, and their hearts, plus white pepper. The secret of its fantastic flavor is that it is dried for between 90 and 130 days. There is garlic in this one, and two slices of it at eventide will make passengers move upwind of you on morning buses.

Now. Let us build a noble sandwich with Rath's specialties.

Go to your friendly neighborhood delicatessen and get, oh, about one-half pound of each Rath product. Buy some cherry tomatoes, or some Italian ones, and some scallions and/or onions. Stop by the bakery to buy either one twenty-four-inch loaf of French bread, or one cane-sized loaf of Italian bread.

133

Use the latter as a cane as you stride from the delicatessen to your humble abode. This bread must be absolutely fresh. So fresh that you will be able to pull hunks out of it after you have slit it.

Put all your hunks of hard and dried Rath sausage through your slicer, or get out your best knife and slice them as thin as you can without cutting your fingers. Place all these slices neatly on a nice brown board, and expose them to room temperature while you are making this dressing.

To about 2-ounces of salad oil and one of vinegar (red, if you have it, but white will do), add one-half teaspoonful of marjoram, one-half clove of garlic which you have smashed with the flat side of a cleaver, one-half teaspoonful of garlic powder, one-half teaspoonful of oregano, a pinch or two of basil, a *tiny* pinch of tarragon, a little thyme and some sage. By now, the oil and vinegar will be so overloaded that you will probably have to put in more oil. Do not fret. Put in more oil, about one ounce. Salt thoroughly and add a grind or two of black pepper.

Whisk the daylights out of this. Soon it will begin to get rather cloudy, like the skies over Glasgow. Keep on whisking. Taste it. It should now begin to taste the way Mrs. Manganaro's sauce tastes. You may pour in, if you wish, about one ounce of good stout Chianti.

Your long loaf or loaves have been split lengthwise. You have plucked out the excess bread—for what you are interested in here is the crust. Save the innards for fowl stuffing. Pour the dressing all over the bread, using a pastry brush for spreading it around. Spread it generously.

Spread the bread first with rich butter—not too heavily, please—and then with Hellman's mayonnaise. Lay down on each side of the bread, some watercress which has been soaked and drained on cloth or paper towels. Over that, lay one or another of Rath's sausages which have been sliced so thin that you can almost see through them. After you have gotten down two layers, put in a layer of thinly sliced tomatoes.

Now come two more layers of different kinds of sausage,

134

and, on top of that, some uncooked cauliflower, sliced as thin as you can. At this point, it might be wise to add some more of the dressing.

Then two more layers of different sausage. On top of them, some provolone, the real thing, please. Have the proprietor of an Italian grocery slice it as thin as the sausage and tomatoes. Next, cucumbers, then two more layers of sausage. More dressing, ladled over lightly. Finally, onions.

What you have done here is created a submarine sandwich that would make the Manganaro people tremble in anticipation. Not really a submarine—a *hero*. Lay some fresh cabbage leaves over it, gently close, stick and fasten with small skewers, and serve. It needs no accompaniment, except possibly wine or beer. A man I know drank milk with it one night and he was never invited to my house again.

People have been known to add anchovies to this monster. They are very good, but unless they are used sparingly, they will take over from the Rath sausages, the onions, and the tomatoes. Capers are also good if used sparingly. Chopped fresh parsley goes well with the onions.

I made this mammoth sandwich one night for guests, all of whom were prepared to rush me to Waterloo and make me a new Napoleon. "You could beat any Duke that Rath might have," they said. I agreed but demurred. I will not go to Waterloo, Iowa, to engage in combat with the Rath people. I will go to shake their hands, for their sausages deserve this unashamed, unsolicited tribute—they are among the best now being manufactured on the North American continent.

RILLETTES. The late Alice B. Toklas, the close friend of the late Gertrude Stein, left two splendid, not to say two rather eccentric, cookbooks before her death. The flyleaf of *The Alice B. Toklas Cookbook* says: "Throughout many rich years, through two World Wars, Miss Stein wrote and talked, Miss Toklas cooked and cooked—both living life to the full." Miss Toklas kept Miss Stein well fed, often on exotic items, one of which was a jarred sausage called *rillettes*.

135

To make this, she ground up two pounds of pork breast. The meat was simmered in one pound of lard, and to it was added one tablespoonful of salt, one teaspoonful of pepper, and one of poultry seasoning. This simple mixture was simmered over a very low flame for about four hours, then removed from the fire and allowed to cool. Then Miss Toklas ladled the sausage into jelly glasses which were covered with paper or sealed with the excess lard. In a cool cellar, this sausage will keep for months. Splendid as sandwich filling.

ROBIN'S EGGS GOLDENROD. One of the most amiable fellows I know is Ernest Beyl of San Francisco, who lives in a small but seemingly spacious apartment overlooking San Francisco Bay. I get a little work done while visiting Beyl, but not much. Ernie loves to drink, shop, cook, eat, and listen to jazz. He says he likes to play tennis, too, but has never been guilty of that in my presence.

He has made up some good recipes in his day, this Beyl, Robin's Eggs Goldenrod being one of them. Because he is editor of a magazine for which I write occasionally, I would not dare paraphrase him, so here is the recipe in his own words.

"I call this 'Robin's Eggs Goldenrod' because I made it for Robin one Sunday morning when she was sore at me for something I had or hadn't done. Anyhow, here goes.

"On a nice hot plate, you put a piece of buttered toast which should be fairly stiff before buttering. Then you line up, close together, a row of fine small pork sausages that you have just cooked and then browned. Over the top of the sausage and toast, you pour about one half of a can of Aunt Penny's White Sauce—or make your own white sauce if you feel so inclined.

"Now you take the yolk of a hardboiled egg and, if you have an egg slicer, run it through that. Otherwise, put it in a tea strainer and jam it through. The yolk will come out of the strainer looking like little yellow ants.

"Take the crumbled yolk and sprinkle it all over the top of the white-sauce-covered sausages and toast. You could sprinkle a few drops of sherry or red wine over the sausages when you are lining them up on the toast. Only a few drops, though. No heavy-handed stuff. Now get to work and chop the white of the egg, very fine, and sprinkle it around the edge of the plate.

"Top all this with paprika and black pepper—unless the sausages are Italian, in which case they already will contain pepper enough. You might add some salt, but probably you already have put some in the white sauce and it won't be necessary. Garnish all this with slivers of tomatoes or the ever-popular parsley, and serve it as fast as you can.

"This will get any wife over a pout. By the time Robin had finished hers, she had forgotten what she was sore about. By the time I had given her a cup of red wine to go with it, she was positively cooing. I went out into the living room and watched the ships in the Bay for a while, wondering what in hell she *had* been sore about."

ROSEMARY KAMM MILLER'S SAUSAGE CASSEROLE. Mrs. Miller of Ephrata, Pennsylvania, is known widely for several of her sausage recipes, as well as for her method of making *metzelsuppe*, which she calls hog maw. Here is the simplest of Mrs. Miller's favorite sausage recipes.

"Make dough as for baking powder biscuits. Roll and cut into pieces four-inches wide by eight-inches long. Take fine-ground sausage, put three or four pieces on the dough and roll up. Press ends together and bake half an hour in 400° oven."

SAUERKRAUT AND SAUSAGE. That fabulous cook of Columbia, Pennsylvania, Mrs. Oscar (Ruth) Luecke, sent me this fine stewpotter.

Make one-and-one-half pounds of sausage into good-sized balls, about two per person. Brown them lightly. Bring home one large can of sauerkraut from the friendly, or unfriendly, as the case may be, grocer or the delicatessen, or make it yourself.

Carom the sauerkraut into the pot in which the sausage balls have been lightly browning. Add one-half cup of water, as well as a teaspoonful of carroway seeds. If you are feeling experimental, add one teaspoonful of poppy seeds. Sauerkraut needs no salt. Before serving, sprinkle with more carroway and poppy seeds and grind some pepper over the whole thing. Link sausages may also be used with sauerkraut even though Mrs. Luecke insists on loose sausage balls.

Incidentally, this dish can be enhanced by the addition of slivers of calf's head, in which case it must be cooked longer, unless you have parboiled the head for about twenty or thirty minutes. I have found that it is almost impossible to cook sauerkraut too long. Small potatoes may be added to this if they have been parboiled, and small onions, as well. And a bay leaf.

To make this even more elaborate, bits of ham from a left-over roast could be added. Dumplings could be made and dropped in. Also small hunks of Lebanon bologna, or tiny bits of leftover chicken or duck, or even goose.

At the last minute, just before the sauerkraut-covered sausage is taken from the stove, about two good slugs of white wine should be poured in. It should be stirred around, and then the whole thing should be tasted. The seasonings should be adjusted according to your taste. Then more stirring.

Aside the sauerkraut, there should be some mashed potatoes, preferably French's. Take the potatoes and, instead of the liquid recommended on the package, use some of the sauerkraut liquid. This will impart a most beguiling flavor to the potatoes.

Afterthoughts. Pig's jowls, in slivers, can be substituted for calf's head. So can lungs, if they are properly chopped. So can sweetbreads. The sauerkraut is going to overpower them all, anyhow. It can even overpower Spam.

SAUSAGE À LA KING. What would I do without my Winchester Farm Sausage file? Go to Tobin's, I suppose, or to Kunzler's. Some nice man who works for the Winchester Farm people sent me thirteen file cards, each containing a sausage recipe. I cannot pretend that I have tried each one, but I have tried several of them, and they are all reliable. This is an *especially* reliable one.

Take one-and-one-half cupfuls of sausage, pan fry it in chunks, and add one-half cupful of sautéed mushrooms. Add to this mixture, one tablespoonful of chopped green pepper and the same amount of chopped pimento, plus about two cups of cream sauce, salt, pepper, and onion salt. Combine all this and let it heat through. Serve it either on toast or fried noodles.

Another good Winchester Farm sausage recipe, also made with noodles, goes as follows:

Brown about one-and-one-half pounds of small sausages, and when they are done, place half of them in a greased casserole. Cook one four-ounce package of noodles or macaroni. Cover the sausages with about half of the noodles, and then add a package of frozen peas. Next, slice an onion, thinly—one approximately the size of Mr. Magoo's nose. Peel it first, unless you're fond of onion skin. Get three or four fresh tomatoes and slice them and let them join the other ingredients. Salt and pepper to taste. Add the rest of the noodles. It's my theory that a person can never have too many noodles.

Now, put the rest of your sausages on the top of the casserole. Cover it tightly and put it into a 350° oven for an hour, perhaps even a little longer.

Winchester says to use canned tomatoes with this one, but I do not agree. The maxim of the good chef is: *Never, ever use canned stuff when you can grab fresh stuff off a grocery counter.* If you do use fresh tomatoes, you'd be protecting yourself, not to say your guests, by adding approximately one-half cupful of water, or perhaps white wine.

Still another sausage dish made with pasta is a kind of sausage-macaroni goulash. The sausages should be halved crosswise and sautéed in a skillet until they are browned. Take them out. Drain off all fat but about three tablespoonfuls. In that fat, brown one cupful of chopped green pepper and one onion about the size of a cup. Do not let this get too brown. Put the sausages back in, add one large can of tomatoes, drained, one cup of sour cream, and one cup of uncooked elbow macaroni, plus salt, pepper, and a tablespoonful of A-1 Sauce. Bring to the boil and then reduce the heat.

Now, stir the whole thing and sprinkle it with dried or fresh parsley, and a small, small, small pinch of oregano. You might find that some basil would go well in it, or some crushed and dried oleander, although the latter is sweetish to my taste. It is also poisonous, says the dictionary.

Winchester Farm recommends its sausage for turkey stuffing, mixed with bread, milk, eggs, parsley, chopped celery and onion, as well as, baking powder, salt and pepper. This is called Frau Meuser's Sausage Turkey Stuffing. They also give a recipe for poultry stuffing made with sausage and corn, using two boxes of frozen whole-kernel corn, one-half pound of fried loose sausage and a diced onion, *after* the sausage is browned and all but three tablespoonfuls of grease has been poured off. Stale bread crumbs, the corn, poultry seasoning and salt and pepper go into this and then it is allowed to simmer for a while before being stuffed into the bird.

SCALLOPED POTATOES AND SAUSAGE. This dish does not require *much* work, but it asks for some. It is a nice one-dish meal that can satisfy a group of six and leave all the guests burpingly happy.

Peel—oh, how I hate to peel potatoes!—about six potatoes. They should be good-sized spring ones—the kind that come up from Florida or out of the western states, although you can use Idahos or other baking-types. Get all of the eyes out of them, and then slice them thinly.

A stout casserole should be hauled out—an earthen one, a Corning one, or some other kind that will not crack. While you are looking for this vessel, fry about eight or ten links of sausage, cut up and decased. Or about one-half pound of loose sausage. It should be plain old country sausage, seasoned with salt and pepper.

The oven should be up to around 375°. The casserole should be greased with some of the sausage fat, swabbed around with a paper towel. A layer of the potatoes should now be put down. On top of this should go a layer of the sausage, link-cut-up or loose. Some dried or fresh parsley should now be sprinkled or cut in.

Chop an onion, or slice one thinly. The size of this onion is entirely up to you. In any event, the onion should be placed over the parsley. Now a single clove, uncrushed, should be dropped in the direct center of the dish. Some cayenne should be sprinkled on—a very small amount. Plus two pinches of salt.

Put another layer of the potato slices on top of this layer, then some more sausage bits, or crumbs, and then about one-eighth of a pound of butter, in small cubes. Then a little more salt and cayenne. By this time, you should have enough potatoes left over to have a final layer of them on top. Put some of the remaining sausage on top of them. Sprinkle the whole thing with paprika.

Pour a quart of milk over the whole thing. This operation will alarm you. You will think you are spoiling your layered arrangement. You are not spoiling it. Keep pouring on the milk until all the ingredients are inundated.

Put a lid, or a cover, or a sheet of aluminum foil, over the casserole, and put it into that oven to bake for about forty-five minutes. Yank it out then, and sprinkle it with some kind of

141

cheese—Parmesan, Romano, shredded Gouda, or some other sharp cheese. Put it back in to cook, uncovered, for fifteen minutes or more.

At this point, some people lay bacon strips or bits of leftover boiled ham across the top. It seems to me that the sausage already has imparted a sufficient flavor of pork to the dish, and that this is an unnecessary move. Some people also put the dish under the broiler after the cheese has been added, but this, too, is an unnecessary move. The cheese will get brown all by itself, and needs only the oven heat to make it that way. Onion rings may be strewn over the top for this last part of the operation.

Just before serving, the casserole should be sprinkled liberally with paprika.

This makes a splendid main dish, but people with hearty appetites often want something more on the side. I would suggest a stout green salad with perhaps some tomato slices, plus a simple oil-and-vinegar dressing. French or Italian bread can be used to mop up the milk-and-cheese mixture after the diner has had his fill of sausage and potatoes.

I fear this is not for people who count calories carefully—but, after all, practically no sausage dish is.

SCHNITZ UND KNEPP UND SAUSAGE. Sometime, somewhere, someday, someone ought to compile a dictionary of that strange amalgamation of German-Dutch-English called Pennsylvania Dutch, which is spoken by the Amish, the Mennonites, and even by the Scotch-Irish and English who settled in Lancaster County at about the time the Indians were still using bows and arrows.

As far as I know, there are glossaries of this antique tongue, but none tells me the answer to how one spells the word for dried apples. Some say *snitz*, some say *schnitz*. I prefer the latter, for it looks more like the way the word is pronounced. Fortunately, there is no dispute over the word *knepp*. *Knepp* are dumplings.

Mrs. Kready, that genteel octogenarian, gave me this recipe. It will be rather difficult for people not living in the Lancaster

County area to duplicate, for *schnitz* are sold mainly in Lancaster's famous farm markets. I believe you can get some by writing Lancaster's mayor, who will turn your letter over to the commissioner of markets, who, in turn, will turn it over to his secretary, who will find some Pennsylvania Dutchman who makes *schnitz*, who will send you some if he happens to remember. This is all very complicated. Perhaps I ought to forget the whole thing.

No, I won't. *Schnitz und knepp und sausage* is too good not to be given an honored place in a compendium of sausage recipes.

Like nearly all sausage dishes, this one is easy, but it does involve some work.

The night before you make the recipe, soak the dried *schnitz* in water. Next morning, grab one pound of sausage for each half-pound of *schnitz* you have soaked. Cut the sausage, which should be smoked back-country type that comes in foot-long lengths, into two-inch pieces. Do not remove the sausage casings. Brown this sausage in butter or lard or bacon grease, and when it is colored, cover it with water and allow it to simmer. Add the *schnitz* to the sausage. Some people change the water just before adding the *schnitz*. I don't.

While the sausages are steaming away, you can make the *knepp*. "About two cups of flour," says Mrs. Kready, "and a bit of salt, and two teaspoonfuls of baking powder, and enough milk to make a soft batter."

This batter should be dropped by the tablespoonful on the boiling sausage and dried apples and, "when it is all," as the Pennsylvania Dutch would say, the pot or pan should be covered and allowed to remain that way until the dumplings look to be done. The only way to tell for sure is to spear one, take it out, and break it. If it looks like soft bread inside, it is done.

What to serve with *schnitz und knepp* is moot. Corn relish is a good bet, if you can find it or if you have put some up during the preceding fall. It should be served in a separate dish. Or pickles, preferably sour ones. Or a side dish of boiled new potatoes. Some people prefer to put the potatoes right in with the dried apples and sausage, but others feel that the dried

143

apples take something from the pure potato flavor. I have known some Lancaster County farm families who, despite my abominable Pennsylvania Dutch, have suffered me to come to lunch or dinner, and have served string beans or fresh-from-the-garden peas, or even, on one occasion, steamed summer squash.

Forget all that nonsense about the Amish and Mennonites loading their tables with seven sweets and seven sours. It simply is not true. No member of the Plain Folk, as they call themselves, would ever be that prodigal. You will get plenty to eat in Amishland, but you will not get seven sweets and seven sours.

SCRAMBLED EGGS AND SAUSAGE. Let us get this clear. There is only one way to make scrambled eggs, and that is in a double boiler. I'm sorry, but I'm obdurate about this.

Put some sausages either under the broiler or in a frying pan, whichever is your usual way. While they are browning, break at least two eggs for each person you will be serving, and put them in a bowl along with one teaspoonful of water for each egg. Get the double boiler simmering along. Whisk the eggs, add chopped or dried parsley, salt and pepper, and perhaps some basil. While you're whisking the eggs, pour in two jiggers of cream.

By now, the top of the double boiler should be rubbed with butter to receive the eggs. Dump them in and put the lid on for about two minutes. Uncover them and begin working with the whisk again. If you like scrambled eggs wettish and soft, they will be done in less than five minutes. If you like them hard and dry, which is downright silly of you, they will take longer.

Now take the sausages from the broiler or the skillet and halve them. Add them to the eggs and serve them, garnishing with tomato slices.

SCRAPPLE. Personally, I loathe scrapple.

Scrapple is the principal character in a dismal cast of night-

144

mares from my childhood, and I cannot eat it today without remembering the hard times of the depression when my father was never without the back of an envelope to figure on. The envelope usually contained a bill. My mother seldom made scrapple at home. She bought it in one of the Lancaster markets and brought it back and cooked it—that is, fried it. It is not hard to make at home. Here is how.

Take one cup of water, one cup of corn meal, stirring the meal gradually into the boiling water along with one-and-one-half teaspoonfuls of salt. While you are frantically stirring this, simmer or fry at least a pound of loose or uncased sausage in a frying pan over a low heat.

The corn meal (you can also use grits or polenta) should cook for about an hour, or until most of the water is gone, or until it gives you a pain in the arm when you stir it. When the sausage is just about done, pour it into the corn or grits mixture. Now you *really* have some stirring to do. Stir the two together, the meat and the sausage, and pour them into a bread-baking pan. Let the mixture cool. Set it into the refrigerator and forget it for a day.

The way most people make scrapple (which usually, and incorrectly, is referred to as Philadelphia scrapple) is to cut the cooled meal and sausage into half-inch slices, dredge it in flour, and forget it again. Scrapple is always getting forgotten, poor beast. Or, you can dip it in egg, then in flour, then in egg again, and fry it that way. But you will have Satan's own time cleaning the pan later. It sticks unless there is a small amount of grease to brown it.

Some cooks contend that scrapple has enough grease in itself to cook. But, in my view, if it is edible, it has been done with a very small amount of oil or grease. Some people grease their frying pans or spiders before putting them away, rubbing the bottoms gently with a rag or paper towel soaked in grease or oil or even butter, and that is often enough for the frying of scrapple. Add a tablespoonful more, if you think it is not enough.

A good many people I know eat sausage links and scrapple

145

together. This, to me, is being redundant because there is already sausage in the mush. Scrapple is far better fried all by itself and served with scrambled eggs, or eggs lightly fried, sunnyside up or over lightly, in a separate pan. You do not need toast with this breakfast dish. The corn meal suffices.

I suppose this may be the first cookbook in the history of cookery-writing that contains a section in which the cook maintains a defiant attitude towards a recipe he is describing. Nevertheless, I must declare that scrapple is not usually fit to eat done as it is usually done. It is greasy, mushy, and altogether unsatisfactory.

SCRAPPLE AS MADE BY SHAKERS. As set out in the *Shaker Cookbook*, edited by Caroline B. Piercy, there is a superior recipe for scrapple which may be more interesting to people who are fond of this abominable alleged delicacy.

Two cupfuls of pork are first boiled in four quarts of water. The meat is drained and about three quarts of the liquid is set aside. The meat is now put through the chopper or grinder or minced with a good stout knife.

Now bring the broth to a boil. Add to it, one-and-one-half teaspoonfuls of salt, one-eighth teaspoonful of sage, the same amount of marjoram, and one-half teaspoonful of pepper. Into the boiling tempest go two cupfuls of corn meal and two of whole wheat flour. And, of course, the ground pork.

The whole thing should be cooked thoroughly for about thirty minutes, perhaps longer, and should be stirred the way a shivering Shaker might do it. It should then be poured into dishes or loaf pans. After it is cold, it can be sliced down and fried in hot fat on both sides until the slices are brown.

I would serve this with apple butter. I would not like it much, or at least not much more than I like the preceding scrapple recipe, but there it is.

SHRIMP AND CRAB SAUSAGE. Yes, yes. Do not recoil, please. This can be a great dish if properly prepared.

Get about three-quarters of a pound of shrimp, preferably

146

the big ones that come out of the Texas gulf. The small ones that are found off the Florida coast will do, but the big ones are better. Boil them in a stock made as follows: one cupful of stale beer that has been taken from a bottle or can that was opened the night before; one bay leaf; one stalk of celery with leaves on it; one coarsely-chopped onion; one sprig of parsley; some paprika; about six or eight black peppercorns.

When this mixture has been boiling furiously, throw in the raw shrimp. They should be boiled no more than five minutes and then removed from their grave. Shell them, being careful of your fingers, for their shells may be tough enough to cut you. Set them aside.

While the shrimp are cooking, pick over about one-quarter of a pound of the best crab meat you can find. Try not to find the canned kind—unless the manufacturer absolutely guarantees that it is fresh from Chesapeake Bay. This is to say *go to your fish dealer*. Try not to buy canned crab in the supermarket.

With a lean, hungry French chef's knife, *hatchet* the shrimp and crab into coarse pieces. Run them through the meat grinder together with the juice of a lemon. Use the finest blade, please. Put these two items through twice, please. Scrape all the delicious pieces out of the grinder and add them to the bowl that has caught the already-ground bits and pieces.

Season the contents of the bowl with a very small pinch of curry powder, about one-half teaspoonful of cayenne, about the same amount of paprika, and three or four drops of Tabasco. Salt it *lightly*.

There is more work ahead, so at this point you will probably need to sit down and relax as you will. Cooks must not be hurried. They must have sustenance while they are waiting for their labors to end.

Put a small piece of uncooked salt pork—about one-eighth of an ounce—through the selfsame grinder that did in the shrimp and crab. Add this to the latter. If it is lean salt pork, fine, but it is my view that if it is practically all fat, so much the better. Mix well.

Before all this, you will have gone to see the butcher and

procured yourself about two feet of bung. Wash this. Pork casings are better. I cannot tell why, except that they *taste* better. Stuff the casings with the crab and shrimp and salt pork mixture.

Once you have the stuffing into the casing, tie it off into sections, each about four inches long. Make good sturdy knots, so that you can cut the sausage with ease when it has finished frying in either oil or butter. Do not use too much of either. About two tablespoonfuls, whichever you use, will be enough for a two-foot sausage of this kind. Coil it in the skillet. Turn it frequently. The idea is to get a decent brown color and not to burn it or allow the skin to pop.

I hate French fried potatoes, ordinarily—and I especially hate the frozen kind which taste like those papier-maché hats sold on Times Square, the ones that have *Doug* and *Bruce* sewn into their front crowns. But if you have a deep-fat fryer, and you are up to the effort of slicing potatoes into strips, you might enjoy them with this.

This seafood sausage can also be made with flounder instead of crab, or with lobster meat instead of shrimp, or even with shad or some other soft and tender fish, such as whiting, provided the fish bones have been tweezered out. Instead of salt pork, loose sausage meat may be used, but its flavor is so assertive, so demonstrable, it tends to kill the flavor you are looking for.

Another fine side dish to serve with this is a mess of snow peas, if you can find them. Only the Amish in Lancaster County (who call them sugar peas) and the Chinese gardeners in the west (who call them snow peas) ever grow them. They do come frozen, however, which might help your search.

SKILLET-BAKED SAUSAGE. The wonderful thing about prepared sausage, as Tobin, Rath, Kunzler and other manufacturers are always saying to us, is that it is so handy and easy to do. I have said that a few times in here myself. I may even say it again for the benefit of those who are not reading line-by-line but skipping around.

It most often comes smoked or cured. It needs hardly any preparation beyond being put in a baking dish or skillet. It needs practically no seasoning, for its makers have already taken care of that. All it needs is what any human needs: appreciation.

One of the dishes of which I am fond is called a Sausage Skillet Bake from the file-card of the estimable Winchester Farm people.

First, cook two cupfuls of rice. Do not use the instant kind. Stick to the real thing. While the rice is cooking, put the sausages, links or loose, into an iron or glass vessel that can go into the oven. Add to it about four tablespoonfuls of chopped onion, the finer the better. Let the sausage and onion become intimate on top of the stove.

Pour off the oil drippings. The cooked rice should be done by the time the sausage is. Add it to the sausage and onion. Take a good-sized can of cooked tomatoes. If you have any sense, you will use the kind you find in an Italian grocery. Drain them first, for you will want to save the juice for drinking later.

Pour the canned tomatoes over the sausage, onion, and rice mixture which is now fulminating in its skillet, or casserole, or whatever it is. Add about two tablespoonfuls of diced green pepper—very well diced. Now add two tablespoonfuls of ketchup.

Now be generous with the salt and sparing with the pepper. If it is possible, use a ground mixture of black and white peppercorns. Put in some chopped pieces of parsley and a sliver or two of whole nutmeg, or a pinch of it if you have it already ground. Some powder of cloves, or some whole cloves, should be added. Then a whole clove of garlic, impaled on a toothpick, so you can fish it out when the whole thing is done. Hardly anybody likes to bite into a whole clove of garlic. Stir the mixture again. Cover it. Put it in an oven of about 300°. This dish should go for about thirty minutes.

On the side, serve some vegetable such as steamed spinach, mustard greens, okra, or, possibly, fresh scallions that have been cleaned and touched daintily with poultry seasoning. Or braised leeks, or perhaps even something as assertive as boiled cabbage, cut up after it has been boiled and given a tablespoonful of carroway seeds and another of poppy seeds.

SPINACH AND SAUSAGE. Let's get all the tired spinach jokes out of the way before we go into this. All the ones like "I say it's spinach, and I say the hell with it." Spinch—my market friends call it that—tastes good. It is so rich in iron and various other minerals that it would be idiotic of me to try to chronicle them here.

Take some spinach and boil it for a time. It should be soft by the time you take it out of the pot. After that, drain it on a towel and then put it through the grinder. Simmer veal bungs in salt water.

Now take about two pounds of veal and put that through the grinder, using the coarse blade. Remove the coarse blade, substitute the fine one, and put the spinach and the veal through the fine one together. Smell this mixture. Salt and pepper it, put in a very, very small pinch of oregano, and the same amount of poultry seasoning. Smell it again. Add some monosodium glutamate if you feel that is necessary. I always feel that it is.

Get out the veal bungs you have been simmering. Allow them to cool, all of them. Wash them off a few more times, also in salt water.

("God! Sausage-making is a time-consuming process!" I often cry it out in the dawn. Sometimes I cry it out in the afternoon, too. And the evening.)

Attach the bung to the business end of the grinder, and grind the veal and spinach through it again. Grind slowly, please. From time to time, taste it again, to make sure that you have put in the proper seasonings. Some grind in a small amount of chives. Others add more pepper. Until you have made this sausage a few times, you are not prepared to decide how much of what you will put in.

Tie the sausage up in the usual way in about six-inch lengths. If you have a smokehouse, hang them up to smoke. If you do

150

not have a smokehouse, hand them to some small son and tell him to hang them in a cool, dry place. Or, at least, a cool place. If you have a cave in your neighborhood, that will do. Allow the links to hang for at least two weeks. Don't be depressed if they look greenish. They usually do. But this is normal.

To cook these little lads, melt a heaping tablespoonful of butter in a large frying pan. When it is turning brown, throw some chopped onion into it. Do not let the butter get brown. Put the onion in when the butter is still golden, and then salt and pepper it, perhaps adding a pinch of parsley.

Throw the spinach sausages into the butter and turn the heat down. Let them expostulate in the pan for about fifteen minutes, turning them as often as you think about it—say, perhaps, once every four or five minutes. They should be browned on all sides.

Aside them, in a separate pan or skillet, cook some red cabbage. This is easily done. Get a head of cabbage, the red kind, core it, clean it, and shred it, using either knife or grater. Put it all into the colander and run water over it, being sure to wash it well.

Lave the red cabbage first, with some red wine or vinegar. Slice in an onion—a small one, about the size of a child's croquet ball. Slice in only about half of it. Give the rest to some cat you loathe.

Two tablespoons of sugar go in next. More salt. The amount depends upon you. Some ground cloves—but only a small amount—and some nutmeg. All this should be permitted to simmer over a very low flame until it is done. It is advisable to start the cabbage well in advance of the sausage, preferably *not* using a pressure cooker to speed things up.

Cook the red cabbage until it is soft, but still more or less crisp. Cabbage, especially the red kind, does not give up easily, not even after being sliced into strips or shredded.

With the sausages browned into a state of docility, and the cabbage cooked to a state of near-perfection, put two of the *wurst* on each plate with a large spoonful of cabbage nestling up to it. Apart from this, place one fairly green plum, a slice

151

of orange, and a slice of lemon. Around the dish, strew slices of cucumber, the thinnest slices you can manage. Put two anchovy-stuffed olives on each place-serving, and the meat of one or two preserved walnuts. If you have a roast wild duck handy, one that has been getting cold—not to say old—in the refrigerator for days, sliver it, and lay the small strips over the sausage, and a small amount over the cabbage, too.

The spinach in the sausage and the flavor of the red or white cabbage, will go well together. They will prove to be digestible and nourishing at the same time. If they start to fight, the duck will separate them and make them friends again.

SQUASH AND SAUSAGE.   For some reason, I never have any luck growing my own acorn squash. I don't know why. It may be that I plant them too late, or too early, or something. This is no real worry, for they seem to be plentiful and cheap all the year around, which is a great advantage, as I happen to like them almost unreasonably. In fact, my heart leaps up as I behold this gift of God.

To make sausage and acorn squash, get two of the latter and scrub them well. These vegetables often pick up a good deal of dirt in the course of maturing. Cut them in half, lengthwise. With a sharp spoon, scrape out the seeds and pulp in the middle of each half.

Into the shells you have manufactured with your knife, pour about two tablespoonfuls of melted butter combined with one quarter cupful of honey which has been mixed well with your whisk, or fork, or whatever you use for mixing up stuff. The acorn halves should be baked in about one-half inch of water for about a half hour in a 400° oven with the cut sides up.

While the halves are baking, you should be browning eight link sausages, or one-half pound of loose sausage meat, in a skillet, turning often as you go, and not allowing them to get too crusty.

No seasoning is needed here. The sausage brings its own on this trip. If the links are small, cut them in half and place two in each acorn half. If the sausage is loose, spoon in as much as you think each guest will eat, perhaps leaving some aside in a separate dish.

Now put the stuffed squash back into the oven, which then is turned down to 325°, and put some more water in the baking pan. Bake for about fifteen more minutes.

Take out and serve with whatever vegetable you feel like eating. I would suggest carrots, steamed with parsley, or corn, also steamed, or, if it's Niblets, right out of the can and simply heated. No potatoes with this one, please. You may like a green salad on the side. I don't. But then, I am self-elected President of the American Salad-Hating Society.

This acorn squash dish can also be done with frankfurters. Go through the same procedure as you would with sausage, slicing one frankfurter into each acorn half. Because frankfurters will need more flavoring-up than sausage, pour a mixture of honey and melted butter over them, and sprinkle each squash with salt, pepper, and about one-quarter teaspoonful of brown sugar. Also, brush the frankfurters with mustard, Colman's dry mustard, if you want this dish to be especially mouth-burning. If you do use Colman's, use it rather sparingly.

You can also make this dish with summer squash, zucchini, and even with eggplant or a baked potato. It can be topped with any number of cheeses, even though I think cheese spoils the delicate flavors of both the sausage and the squash.

SUMMER SQUASH AND SAUSAGE. Mrs. Maudie Bates, wife of Kenneth O. Bates, one of the fostering fathers of Armstrong Cork, first turned me on to the summer-blooming squash —the flat, round, quietly fluted kind which is greenish-white on top with a belly as white as a shark's.

This squash will grow, if permitted, to the size of at least a ten-inch pie plate, at which time it has to be peeled before it is cooked. It is far better to raise it yourself, and to grab it off the vines when it is still about the size of a half-dollar. That was the size it was when Mrs. Bates first served it to me and to her son Steve who, before his death, was one of my closest friends, one of the most talented young directors in the New York theater.

Maudie Bates introduced me to this squash the day she and her husband returned home from a trip to Europe. If the Bates' saw the mayhem Steve and I had done to their home in their absence, they did not mention it.

"I hope you two had a good time," Maudie said, and tore off to one of the city markets. She came back, bearing several large brown paper bags, one of which contained around two pounds of baby Pattypan squashes, which the English call vegetable marrow, and we sometimes call scalloped squash. Nobody I know ever eats crookneck squash, another breed.

Maudie produced these tiny squashes with pride, and went on to boil them gently in milk, draining them, and then adding butter. After which, we ate them and sang choruses of *You're a Winner, Maudie Bates.*

Having been taught the true values of this splendid squash, I began to experiment with it. First, I tried using it with tomato paste, or fresh tomatoes, as a side dish to broiled hamburger. Good, but the tomato paste killed the taste of the squash. Then I tried it as a side dish to broiled fish without tomato sauce. The fish killed it, too.

I was determined to discover what meat could be made to go with that delicate flavor, and presently I hit upon sausage. I took about eight small links of the unsmoked plain pork kind, browned them, poured off all but about two tablespoonfuls of the sausage grease, and then made a roux of the remaining sausage oils, and poured that over the links.

In a side dish, I did the baby squash just as Maudie Bates had, using a little water and milk, and about one-eighth of a pound of butter. Salt and pepper on both the sausages and the squash, of course. When the squash seemed done, I threw it on top of the cooking sausage, covered the whole thing, and let it go.

This thing could be done in a casserole. Add more roux and take care that it doesn't get too thick. The sausage will not kill the taste as long as you keep the squash mainly on top of the

154

pot. Sausage must be a frustrated soul. It always tried to slay whatever it is being cooked with. But it never quite succeeds.

This dish should be seasoned with nothing more than salt and pepper, as I have mentioned above. I know people in Lancaster County who would do me in just for mentioning salt and pepper. Maudie Bates, for one.

TOAD IN THE HOLE. I don't know where Mrs. Wallace Brook of Manheim, Pennsylvania, got this recipe. It does not begin with "take one fresh toad" nor does it ever include a toad in its ingredients.

It begins with "Make a Yorkshire pudding kind of thing—eight tablespoonfuls of flour, one beaten egg, and a dash of salt. Fold in sausage links which have been cut into one-inch pieces, and bake the whole mess in a 400° oven for about three-quarters of an hour—or until the pudding is set and brown." These amounts, according to Mrs. Brook, can be varied for the number of servings required.

Mrs. Brook adds this postscript: "This is a very satisfying main course meal." Beside it, I would serve coined cucumbers with oil and vinegar sauce, topped with chopped egg and minced onion, with perhaps a little parsley and a tiny pinch of oregano. This may be mixed beforehand, in which case you will come out with a quick-and-easy *vinaigrette* sauce for the ice-cold cucumber slices. The cucumbers can be slivered lengthwise, of course. But if you do that, you should in conscience peel them first.

TOMATOES CAPPED WITH SAUSAGES. Another recipe from the indefatigable Jones Dairy Farm.

Get six or eight or ten tomatoes, as many as you think you may need, allowing one for each guest. Take off their stems and halve them crosswise. Spread the cut side of each of these halves with prepared mustard. I use Gulden's. French's is fine. Colman's is too strong. Top each tomato half with one-half of a tablespoonful of minced onion, a few dashes of Lea & Perrins, and sprinkle them all with some sugar and salt.

156

Put the tomatoes and the Jones sausages side by side under a low broiler heat. If you happen to be cursed with an electric stove, this will be impossible. Your only choice will be to place the sausages and tomatoes down in the oven, as far away from the broiler as you can get them.

Soon the sausages will begin to snarl and crackle, sounding as though they were planning to have the cook guillotined. The tomatoes will be meekly going to their ultimate fates, uncomplaining. Turn the sausages a few times to make sure they are browning evenly. They will continue to sputter. I would advise —and so would the Jones family—that the sausages should not be pricked in this recipe. Gently turn with a wooden spoon, being sure not to allow it to catch fire.

This initial broiling process should take about seven minutes, the dear old Joneses say. It probably should take a little more than that—ten, perhaps, or twelve minutes. Now place two sausages on each tomato half. The Jones family says *one*, but although they make sausages like dervishes, they evidently do not realize how good their own are. They are skimpy with them. Put *two* on each tomato.

Broil this for another seven minutes, first sprinkling a little fresh or dried parsley on the tomatoes. Some cooks I have known have used oregano. I would not. Jones sausages are already well-seasoned and they need nothing more than the stuff you have already put on the tomatoes.

When you haul all this out of the oven, you will already have made some mashed potatoes. Put a good spoonful of them on each plate, with a well in it made with your wooden spoon. Into each well, you will pour some of the formerly indignant, now subdued, drippings from the pan. But first, you must make a gravy of the drippings.

To the drippings, add one small 6-ounce can of mushroom bits and pieces, a couple of teaspoonfuls of cornstarch or flour, no more than one ounce of milk, some pepper and salt and parsley, and the faintest touch of rosemary or basil. And dash in some sherry or bourbon. The Jones family does not recommend the addition of spirituous liquors. I do not know if they use them at all. I use them all the time, when my mother isn't looking.

Lima beans on the side of this dish, if you are making an elaborate breakfast or lunch. And corn bread, perhaps. My God, I think I will go and make some now.

VENISON SAUSAGE. The hardest part of this recipe is shooting a deer. The way to do this is to go with my great-uncle, Ambrose Archibald Cauller, to Cain or Potter counties in Pennsylvania. He gets a deer nearly every late autumn and usually gives me some meat.

It does not matter what cut he offers. It nearly always needs marinating, which is not hard duty. All that has to be done is to put the venison in a good sturdy crock and to marinate it in wine which has been dosed with two bay leaves, a dozen peppercorns, about a tablespoonful of sage or thyme, plus a cut-up and scraped carrot, a couple of stalks of de-stringed celery, and an onion the size of a No. 10 Downing Street door knob.

The meat should be permitted to sweat and ferment in this marinade for at least four days. If you are patient enough, or if you have shot your own deer and have been eating steaks, chops, etc., you will permit it to marinate longer. Skim the marinade every once in a while, please. Penicillin may form if you are not careful. The crock, I forgot to mention, should be covered with a good-sized hunk of cheesecloth, and the meat weighted with a washed stone.

The hour comes. Go to the butcher and buy some casing. I prefer pork casings. Some people like beef casings better. Some purists hold out for veal casings—why, I cannot tell.

When you feel that the venison has had its benison from the marinade, grind it. Then grind it again with cumin, mace, dry mustard, and shredded bay leaves. Let the grinder take care of the peppercorns. Salt it a bit. Now put it through the grinder again with—if it weighs, say, two pounds—about one-half of a pound of either pork fat or well-fatted fresh pork. If you cannot get either of these, good sturdy smoked bacon, Jordan's preferably, will do.

Put it through the grinder a third time. Use the finest cutting blade you have. Take the meat out of the bowl into which you have ground it and stuff it into the casings.

This is strong meat. Some like it plain, some like it smoked. That is entirely a matter of taste. The links ought to be tied so that they are about five or six inches long.

Venison sausages are cooked like any others—started in a little water and allowed to simmer when the water is gone. They should be pricked so that the pork fat can run out and torture them. The kitchen blower or deodorizer ought to be turned on or the place will smell for days as though a herd of deer has just run through, pursued by my Uncle Brose.

While the sausages are behaving as fiercely as they can, you can take a cupful of the marinade, strain it, thicken it with flour or cornstarch, and allow it to simmer gently. I have often added slices of pared and cored apple to it, and I have known some people who have added dried prunes or apricots.

The venison sausages will be ready to eat in about twelve minutes. (While you are waiting, you can have a drink of dandelion wine.) Serve very hot, pouring the thickened marinade over your sausage. Grits or mashed potatoes go well on the side. Some put mustard and/or pickles. I never do. I like the assertive taste of venison and wish my Uncle would go hunting more often.

WAFFLES AND SAUSAGE, ETC. Get one of those packages of Aunt Jemima frozen waffles and permit them to thaw a bit. Now, take out a package of Jones Farm sausages and put them in a skillet or spider with about one-half inch of water.

While the water is cooking off, and the sausages are beginning to brown, slice two tomatoes. Open a very small can of Dole pineapple. Put the waffles either into the toaster or under the broiler and wait until they are done. Edge the waffles with the browned and cooked sausages and put a thin slice of tomato in the center of each waffle. Allow two waffles for each guest. Set some pineapple on the side of each plate. Crushed pineapple is better, especially if it is mixed with Major Grey's Chutney.

All this should be laved with Vermont maple syrup, the purest kind, if you can get it. If you can't, the syruped-down Vermont Maid will do. Or molasses, although you will not like it much. Or honey will do.

If you do not have any sausage on hand, you can improvise by grinding a slice of ham or a can of Spam and laying that on top of the waffles. Or you can use country pudding, that marvelous sausage-like mixture found in markets tended by Amish and Mennonite farmers. This, too, can be spread over the waffles. Chopped onions, or diced celery, or water chestnuts, can be added to the pudding, which comes to you hard and melts down into what seems to be a muddy mass but is really delicious.

The pudding is made from the ears, cheeks, jowls and some of the neck meat of the pig, and sometimes the farmers get a little careless and allow a bristle or two to get in. This is no great problem if you've got a supply of toothpicks handy.

If you do use pudding on waffles, set the syrup aside, or use it sparingly. Good on the side are oranges, pineapple, diced pears or tart sliced apples. I once knew a lady who cut up a persimmon and set that on the side. Another one used currant jelly, another strawberry jam, and yet another black raspberry jam.

If you haven't got Aunt Jemima's frozen waffles lying around your friendly freezer, and do own a waffle iron, it is no great chore to make them yourself.

For six waffles, sift about one-and-a-quarter cups of cake flour, and sift it again with three teaspoonfuls of baking powder, one-half teaspoonful of salt, and one tablespoonful of sugar. Now beat three eggs and put into them anywhere from two to six tablespoonfuls of gently melted butter or the same amount of Wesson or any other salad oil. Butter is better. Do not use margarine.

Add about one-and-a-half cupfuls of milk to the egg mixture. Pour this into the sifted mixture. Pour the whole thing into your blender or into a bowl in which you can use either a whisk or a hand-operated mixer. When it is well-mixed and is producing bubbles, it is ready to go to the pre-heated waffle iron. It is easier to pour from a pitcher.

WALNUTS AND SAUSAGE. Mrs. Laura Immel, who lives in what used to be known as the Cabbage Hill section of Lancaster, sent me this fine recipe. I tried it and found it excellent.

Mrs. Immel takes about a pound of fresh, loose sausage meat and combines it with one cup of seedless raisins. She pours one pint of boiling water over that mixture and adds one pound of brown sugar. (I never put in that much; I use more like three-quarters of a pound.) She then pours in one cup of molasses and one teaspoonful each of cinnamon, ground cloves and baking powder which has been dissolved in "a little" hot water. In then, goes one cup of shelled English walnuts.

All this gets mixed together and then four cups of flour are

162

gradually added. "Add about one heaping tablespoonful if the mixture is not stiff enough," Mrs. Immel said to me in her letter. "Add all together, mix well again, and pour into a tube pan." A lady I know says a tube pan is the kind of pan you make angel food cake in. Live and learn, I always say. (I frequently make up phrases like that in the mornings to spring on friends at lunch.)

Mrs. Immel, who does not say how you pour something that is supposed to be stiff, bakes this cake in her tube pan for anywhere from an hour to an hour-and-a-half at 250°. Meanwhile, she goes about her housework, comforted by the pleasant wafts of odor from the kitchen.

Meanwhile, while picking up around the house, she takes time to make icing for her sausage cake. Down from the cupboard comes one cup of confectioner's sugar which she works into about three-ounces of cream cheese. To this, she adds one-and-one-half tablespoonfuls of cream or milk, beating it all gradually. Then in goes one teaspoonful of vanilla and one-half teaspoonful of cinnamon.

When the sausage cake is done, it comes out of the oven looking as though the Black Baker of Vienna had done it with his own hands. Mrs. Immel then ices it liberally and sets it off somewhere to cool.

The cake, when finally served, resembles those that can be bought along the streets in Berlin, Munich, Frankfurt and other German cities. Because of the sweetness of the icing, it should be served for dessert. Without icing, it makes a delicious meal as a first course. Or a second one, if you are having soup and fish first.

The European custom of serving appetizers, soup, fish, and then an entree, followed by dessert and cheese, with wines or champagnes or beers throughout, is the reason that people from *Mitteleuropa* are, on the average, twenty percent heavier than Americans. People from Lancaster County, it seems to me, average forty per cent heavier than other Americans, yet they live on and on and on.

WELLER'S WILLOW STREET SAUSAGE CASSEROLE.

I never looked on tiny Willow Street, Pennsylvania, with much favor. I do now, though, because Mrs. William A. Weller lives there and she sent me a fine recipe for a sausage casserole which I gather is standard food in that splendidly unsophisticated rural Pennsylvania Dutch town.

Take two-and-one-half cupfuls of filling cubes (I think she means dry bread made into cubes), two or three small diced potatoes, one package of frozen peas, and one-and-one-half pounds of loose sausage meat.

"Mix filling cubes as you would make filling for a fowl," said Mrs. Weller in her letter. "Mix together with potatoes, peas, and about half of the sausage meat, and put into a greased casserole. Put remaining sausage on top of casserole. Bake at 350° for about an hour, or until potatoes are soft. I cover my dish for about three-quarters of an hour, then take the lid off. You also can use sausage in links, but it is better with the sausage meat loose."

WILTED LETTUCE AND SAUSAGE DRESSSING.

Get a good crisp head of lettuce, preferably iceberg, wash it and dry it. Cut it up into bite-sized pieces. Take about eight or ten good pork sausages and sauté them in a skillet over low heat for between twelve and fifteen minutes, turning them often to make sure they are evenly browned. These sausages should not be parboiled first. Whether or not you prick them depends upon your temperament.

Take the sausages off the sautéeing skillet and drain them. Reserve about eight tablespoonfuls of the fat from the sausages and mix it with two tablespoonfuls of lemon juice. Add one-half teaspoonful of salt and two of granulated sugar. Put the lettuce pieces into a bowl. Cut up the sausage links into one-inch bits. Pour all the dressing over them, and then toss as though you were a *jai alai* player.

This makes a sumptuous lunch. Serve either some pickled beets or some raw tomato slices, salted and peppered, on the side.

WÜRSTE VON KALBSGEKRÖSE. The most difficult thing about this item is learning to pronounce its name. It is virtually unpronounceable if you are an American—unless, of course, you were born in Milwaukee, Cincinnati, St. Louis, or Lancaster County.

The sausage itself is not hard to make if you can persuade a butcher to procure some calf's mesentery for you. This is a part of calf's gut which surrounds the stomach, a kind of membrane which is seldom sent by butchers to shops in this country. If you manage to get hold of some, a fine sausage can be made.

The mesentery—a couple of pounds—should be washed thoroughly, set in salt water, and blanched. Pour off the blanching water and cook the mesentery in white vinegar for six or seven minutes. Now pour off the vinegar and cook the stuff in a *court-bouillon* (and if you don't know how to make that, look it up in some other cook book). The *court-bouillon* treatment should last about ten minutes.

Remove the mesentery and chop it into very small bits. Put the chopped cubes, each about one-quarter-of-an-inch square, into a bowl. Add salt and pepper, nutmeg, two fresh eggs, and three-quarters of a cupful of good heavy cream for every two pounds of mesentery. Mix this with your hands or with a wooden spoon and stuff into pork casing, tying each sausage off at about ten-inches. These sausages are best when first poached, taken out and drained, and fried in butter until brown.

Y ET ANOTHER SAUSAGE LOAF. This recipe, forwarded to me by Mrs. Elwood H. Keagy, who gave me the one for Sausage Rolls, is far from complicated and not much different from other sausage loaf recipes in this book, yet worth trying.

One-and-one-half pounds of sausage meat should be married to the same amount of bread crumbs. To that add one tablespoon of grated onion, two of ketchup, two of horseradish, and one-half teaspoonful of what the estimable Mrs. Keagy, and the manufacturers, call "prepared" mustard. I imagine this is the kind you get in a jar. I seldom use anything but dry mustard and, if you use that, use only one tablespoonful.

Moisten this mixture with about one-half cup of milk. Mix thoroughly with a beaten egg, and put the whole mess into a baking pan and then into 350° oven for an hour or an hour and a half. You may wish to drain off some of the grease after the first half hour. Depends on whether you like it moist or dry.

YORK BREAKFAST. I have discovered why the residents of York, Pennsylvania, always look so healthy to me. It is because they eat the York Breakfast, which is not at all hard to put down.

It begins with potatoes, preferably new ones, which have been peeled, set to soak in cold water overnight, and then grated. Four or five of them should make about four cupfuls. Two eggs should be whisked into submission, and two tablespoonfuls of flour should be added to them. Also add two teaspoonfuls of salt, one-half of a teaspoonful of baking powder, and about two tablespoonfuls of chopped onion. All this, added to the potatoes, will make a batter in which a knife will stand firmly. Mix it well with a wooden spoon.

The griddle should be so hot that the cat will leave the house. It should, of course, be greased. Smoked sausages should be sizzling on another griddle or in another frying pan.

Take the potato batter and drop it by wooden spoonfuls on the treacherous griddle. Next to the batter, fry unripe green tomatoes (if you can find them), or red tomatoes, either of which have been dredged in flour. When the sausages have cooked through, they may be placed in a covered dish or casserole and tucked in a warmish oven. The grease in their original pan may be used to make a decent, although not ostentatious, brown gravy to pour over the sausage, potato cakes, and fried tomatoes, to the immense satisfaction of all communicants at the table. Ordinarily, no toast and no muffins are eaten with this.

ZUCCHINI UND KNACKWURST.

This is from Ernest Beyl, who is, as I have said before, a fine cook. (See *Robin's Eggs Goldenrod.*) Try this dish which he invented and hear it in his own mumbling words.

"This is a nice one-dish meal. I make it in one of those good aluminum hotelware frying pans. Cover the bottom of the pan with olive oil. I think about a jigger—two ounces—is enough. Then sauté some chopped onion in that oil. A handful, unless you have a very small hand—in which case, use two handfuls. This ought to be yellow onion.

"Next, make coins of four garlic sausages or knackwurst. Hot dogs will do, but this dish won't be as good if you use them, unless they are the exceptional kind. Throw the coins over the now-transparent onions. While all of this stuff is getting hot, take some zucchini and coin *it* the way you did the sausage. The zucchini should be about the size of the sausage you are simmering. Rinse the zucchini lightly and throw them in the pan with the knackwurst—try to get knackwurst if you can, by all means—and salt and pepper the whole thing. Lightly, please. I sometimes put in a sprinkling of chervil or basil.

"Now put a lid on all this, or cover tightly with aluminum foil. The moisture from the rinsed zucchini will keep the fire from making this stick, but keep that fire low, baby, low. I keep this going on the stove until the zucchini is *al dente.* Not soft, or the entire thing is ruined. I like zucchini crisp. This is a good one-dish meal served with a crisp green salad."

ZUM-ZUM.

One of the greatest sausage restaurants in the world, Zum-Zum, is in the Pan American Building in New York

City, and in various other locations. It has been crowded ever since it opened its doors. One can get a sausage there only at about three o'clock in the afternoon. The *bratwurst, bockwurst,* and plain smoked sausage are superb. More than fifty varieties are sold and they can be carried out for home consumption. I would recommend that readers try *leberwurst mit speck,* which seldom is sold outside German sections of large cities. The *leberwurst mitout speck* is pretty good, too. In fact, there is nothing about Zum-Zum that is bad.

POSTSCRIPT

Thanks are due to Dorothy Jewell, editor and publisher of *The Putnam County Courier*, in which some of this material appeared in shorter form. Thanks also go to the memory of her late father, Willitt C. Jewell, a fine newspaperman, a courageous Democrat in a predominantly Republican community, who will be remembered by those who are following him to his grave with gratitude for his indomitably pure integrity, the like of which is seen all too seldom in American life.

Thanks are due to Mrs. Nellie B. Gehman, despite the fact that she blighted the face of this nation by casting me upon it nearly fifty years ago. So many ladies in Lancaster County contributed recipes, I cannot begin to mention them all. They are mentioned in the text by name.

Sal Farfaglia of Pound Ridge, New York, gave me a great deal of information on Italian sausages and their use in cookery. V. A. Veley of Dayton, Ohio, translated some recipes from the Russian. Both were very kind, and I thank them.

I also wish to express my debt to the various public relations men of innumerable sausage companies, large and small. They are all mentioned by name in the text. Ferdinand Schaller, my friend for many years, was of inestimable help. His patience, as he answered question after question, ensures my being his friend for life. The Kunzler family, in Lancaster, deserves special mention. So does Ken Dean of Hormel. Finally, I want to thank Gerald S. Lestz of Lancaster, to whom—with his family—the book is dedicated.

I cannot thank Elizabeth Woodward Dickinson Benchley enough, for her help is beyond survey. She researched many recipes, pored over an endless number of books, read the manu-

170

script and suggested changes, retyped many pages, and was my diligent collaborator through the months when, at times, it seemed to us that small grains of sausage would begin to come out of our pores. This was odd behavior on her part, for the lady hates sausage and has hated it since childhood. Yet she persevered. She had such rage against the hated meat that she broke a few of my typewriters while persevering. She did persevere; I do now thank her for her so doing.

R. G.

INDEX

173

capicolla (cappo collo), 9
Caruso, Charles, 1
casings for sausage, 4-5, 33, 34,
46, 54, 64, 87, 132, 133, 150,
165; beef, 4, 112, 132; chicken,
125-7; pork, 17, 19, 45, 104,
113, 120, 133, 148, 159, 165;
veal, 150, 159
casseroles, sausage, 22, 23-5, 42,
56, 71, 83, 99, 118, 123, 137,
139, 141, 164
Cassoulet, 42-4
"castoff" animal parts in
sausage, 6
cervelat, 3, 45-6
Chapman, Rodney, 78
cheek meat, 5
cheese with sausage, 29, 72, 75,
76, 92, 101-2, 116, 118, 142
Chef's Salad with Sausage, 46-
8
chicken, 10, 42-3, 124, 125-7;
broth, 73, 77; drumsticks, 77;
livers, 49; wings, 122
Chicken Sausage Hyman
Goldberg, 48-9
Chicken Steamed with Sausage
49-51
chine, 53-4
Chipolata, 51-2
chorizos, 3, 51-2
cider, 129
clams, 78
Corn and Sausage Stuffing for
Poultry, 53
corn meal, 18, 145
cottage cheese, 72-3
Country Sausages as Made by
Mrs. John M. Moore, 53-5
country pudding, 161
court-bouillon, 165
crab meat, 147
Cranberry-Sausage Casserole,
55-7

cream cheese, 163
Creamed Potatoes and Sausage,
57
Cuckolds, 57-8
Cudahy, 12, 78
curry, 116-17, 147

Dumas, Alexandre, père, Le
Grand Dictionnaire de Cui-
sine, 19, 45
Dutch Sausage with Gravy, 59-
60
Dutchman's Stew, 60

Ears, pork, 34
Ebersole, Mrs. Jestena, 95
eggplants, 117
Eggs and Sausages, 61-2
Ella's Sausage and Noodle
Dish, 62-3
Enterprise Grinder, 15
Erickson, Mrs. Herman, 123
Escarola Imbottita, 64
Evans Farms, see Bob Evans
Farms

Fat trimmings, 9
Ferhoodled Sausage, 65-6
Ferrari, Mario, 64
Feuchtwanger, Anton Ludwig,
66
fish, 45, 148
frankfurter, 2, 3, 4, 6, 8, 10, 18,
66-78; casseroles, 72, 75-6, 77-
8; proper cooking of, 68-9;
skinless, 4; soups and stews,
72-3

Königswurste, 112
Kraft Dinner, 84
krakowska, 7-8, 9, 10
Kready, Anna, 124, 142
Kunzler, Christ, 7, 53, 139, 148
Kunzler, Christ, Jr., 30
Kurtz, Mrs. Marvin, 96

La Ideal Market, 52
lamb, 42-3, 85-6, 132
landjaeger, 3, 10
Languedocienne Sausages, 97-8
lard, 54, 55, 136
Lebanon bologna, *see* bologna
leberwurst mit speck, 11, 169
lemon, 78, 110
Lentils and Sausage, 98-100
Liederkranz and Sausage, 100
Lima Beans and Sausage, 102
liver, 2; chicken, 49; chopped, 11; lamb, 85-6; veal, 21
liverwurst, 3, 10
longaniza, 52
Luecke, Mrs. Ruth, 24, 83, 108, 138
Lyon sausage, 103-4, 112

McCullough, Donald, 128
macaroni, 16, 73, 74, 85, 139
Manganaro brothers, 9, 12, 87, 104
meat cuts used in sausage, 5-6
meat loaves, 6
mettwurst, 3
Metzelsuppe, 114, 137
Meuser Meat Loaf, 105
Mexican Frankfurters, 75
milk and cream with sausage, 84, 141, 144, 163

Miller, Rosemary Kamm, 137
Miss Carol's Sausage Concoction, 106-7
Moore, Mrs. John M., 53-4
Morrison, Maxine, 26
mortadella, 3, 9
Mustard Sauce and Sausage, 108

National Pretzel Institute, 128
Nebraska Centennial First Ladies' Cookbook, 123
neck meat, *see* pork
New York City Gourmet Society, 27
noodles, 139
Novotny, Mrs. Dave, 26

Oldenburg *leberwurst,* 12
Omelette with Sausage, 109
orange peel, 2
Our Man In The Kitchen, 48
ox palates, 20
Oxford Horns, 109
Oyster and Sausage Loaf, 110-11

Paraffin for casing, 5
Parisian Saucisson, 112
Partridge Sausages, 112-13
pasta, 92-4
    See also macaroni
pepperoni, 9, 43, 52
Peppers Stuffed with Sausage, 114
Pig Belly a New Way, 114-16
pig's head, 87, 89